NOTES IN BLUE

The Story of a Police Officer, 2nd Edition

D1637538

David Allen Duke

☐

Printed in the United States of America

1st Edition March 2020
2nd Edition October 2020

ISBN 978-1-7347742-1-4

☐

DEDICATION

To the brave men and women of the Atlanta Police Department and to law enforcement officers everywhere.

ACKNOWLEDGEMENTS

The following people deserve a special thanks for helping with this book: To my wife, Linda, who has always supported me with love, encouragement and editing. To my daughter, Rachel, for believing in my idea and helping me keep the narrative interesting. To my friends and family who make life fun and exciting.

Table of Contents

Foreword

All the events in this book are true. The names used are the real names of the people and places unless otherwise stated. When I don't use the real name, it's usually because I did not want to embarrass them for what may have been an honest mistake or a misperception on my part. Sometimes I just forgot the name. I usually omitted names of victims, unless it was an untraceable common name; they've already been victimized enough. Also, some officers didn't want me to use their real name.

The use of quotation marks in the book doesn't mean it's a word-for-word quote, but it is their words as I remember them.

The material covered spans a ten-year period. Most of the calls are from my first few years in the force. The longer I was in Blue, the less I kept notes about my experiences. That's probably because cases I thought were interesting as a rookie became mundane as I got more experience.

I didn't put many dates in the book, because a lot of it is not written chronologically and would probably just be confusing. The Diary sections have dates and are chronological because I wanted to show what a typical shift was like.

I don't generally use profanity, but there is some in this book. Hearing and speaking profanely is a part of being in law enforcement--perpetrators (perps) use it, and many citizens use it. I felt that, in many cases, deleting profanity would not convey to you the actual mood of the moment. Cops often need to use profanity, because it's the only thing some people understand. When faced with a perp holding a gun, you could say, "Police! Put down the weapon." However, under stress that could be mistaken for, "Please, put down the weapon." So, the most effective verbiage often is, "Po-lice! Drop the f@#%ing weapon!" (emphasis on "Po"). In that moment, there probably won't be a second chance; it's best to get the result you want on the first attempt.

The unit in the Atlanta Police Department that investigates officer complaints and misconduct is called the Office of Professional Standards (OPS); however, I refer to it in the book as Internal Affairs because more people are familiar with the latter term. Also, I use the term "Night Watch" in place of the official term used by the Atlanta Police Department, "Morning Watch," in order to avoid confusion.

Enjoy the book; I enjoyed writing it.

Chapter 1. It's a Beautiful Day in Atlanta!

I Want to be the Police

As the son of a career Army officer, it was not a huge stretch when I decided to join the United States Air Force. I took all the requisite exams and qualified to go to flight school; however, as I waited for the Air Force, I became interested in a career in law enforcement. So much so, I applied to the FBI, and enrolled in a part-time police academy conducted by the City of Portsmouth, Virginia.

The academy was conducted two nights a week and on weekends, and I really enjoyed it. I was looking forward to becoming a cop.

Several months into the academy, and with just a couple of weeks to go until graduation, I got a call from the United States Air Force asking if I could report to Officer Training School in three weeks. I immediately said "yes," thinking, "I can always become the police later." In fact, my mind was so made up to go to the Air Force that I turned down an interview with the FBI when they called a few days later.

Off I went to the Air Force, flying helicopters and working some very challenging and rewarding jobs for the next 23 years.

After retirement from the Air Force, I became acquainted with several current and former law enforcement officers. One of my best friends was a retired police officer, and listening to his stories re-ignited my interest. I checked around with some of the local Sheriff's Offices but found that unless I was already state certified, they didn't want anything to do with me. Then a friend told me that the Atlanta Police Department (APD) was desperate for eligible recruits.

I called the APD recruiting office and asked them if they had an age limit for recruits and was encouraged to hear, "As long as you can pass the physical exams, there's no age limit." So, I applied and began my journey in Blue.

Atlanta Police Academy

At 51 years of age I was, at that time, the second oldest recruit to enter the Atlanta Police Department Academy. The physical aspects of the academy didn't concern me (before I arrived) because for the last 35 years I had been going to the gym and running on a regular basis. I was 6 feet tall and weighed 165 pounds, could do more pushups and sit-ups than the average twenty-year-old, and ran a mile in about eight minutes, so I thought the academy would be a breeze. I was sorely, and sadly, mistaken.

One of the worse things about getting older is that your reflexes and speed really slow down. Unfortunately, the physical aspects of policing often require fast reflexes and speed. Long story short, I barely made it through the physical parts of the academy. However, I did have the highest grade- point average and graduated as the valedictorian of my class. The biggest advantage to being the Valedictorian was that I didn't have to listen to someone's boring speech at graduation; I did the boring speech. Here's the speech:

Atlanta Police Department Academy
Class 211 Graduation
July 27, 2010
Officer David Allen Duke

"It's a beautiful day in Atlanta! You got up this morning, didn't you? Some people didn't. So, you're ahead of the game."

Those words, or some derivation thereof, were usually the first words we heard from Senior Patrol Officer (SPO) Barr at roll-call every morning. In fact, if he didn't say those words someone in the class would usually say them after we got back into the classroom. At first, we thought SPO Barr was just playing with our minds, but as the rigor of the academy started to take its toll, we realized that, as Sergeant Butler often says, "There's a message (sic) to his madness." The message was: today is going to suck, but just remember, it could be worse, and tomorrow probably will be.

What you are seeing here tonight is the culmination of a process that started about a year ago for most of us, and a lifetime ago for a couple of us. How long Bautsch? How long Herrick?

211 was a great class. But we were also a unique class. We had 4 professional athletes, 7 current and former military members. And we had some old people. I mean, we had some people who were over 40! I don't know how those guys made it. Well, actually I do; one of them made it by a shoestring (I got hung up by my shoestrings during the obstacle course). We had people from Romania, Puerto Rico, illegal aliens from California, New York, Chicago, and we even had 2 people actually from Atlanta. We were about half white and half black, one of us was pretty and all the others were good looking, half college grads and half not, half politically conservative and half liberal, but none of that seemed to matter because we all became family. And not a dysfunctional family. In fact, I have never in my life seen a group this size with less drama. Sure, we had some squabbles. But in the end, we supported each other, helped each other, and yes, loved each other.

First off, for friends and family here tonight, don't take offense that I call your loved one by only their last name or a nickname. In the academy we really only had time to learn people's last names for at least the first two months, and by that time last name, was, well, their name. Isn't it ironic that the only person in Class 211 with a last name that's a common male first name, Larry, is the only woman in our class? I'm sure we confused more than a few wives and girlfriends when we'd talk about how great Larry was and then go on to say she was also cute and was often like a mother to the class. So, you see, there's no disrespect, it's just the way it was and still is. I mean, I carpooled with Clutter and sat next to him in class for 3 months before I learned his first name was Janice (his real name was actually Jason).

Here's an example of how busy and regimented those first few weeks of the academy were: In about week 8, Officer Jones came in and announced she was giving us a pop quiz. Basically, it was a list of names and we had to write next to the name something about the person. I recognized maybe 4 of the 10 or so names, but only knew for sure that one of them was a fallen APD officer. Well,

we all did pretty bad on the test, and the staff was somewhat upset; you see, those names were on plaques up and down our hallway, commemorating those who had been killed in the line of duty. But we had been running so hard, and were so afraid to look like we weren't hustling that we had never taken the time to read the plaques. I remember someone saying, "you mean we're allowed to stop and read in the hall?" Well, we learned who they were real fast, (after many push-ups and study) and we received a lesson on the dangers of being a police officer.

By the way, any family member who heard the Chaplain's words at our Family Night probably thought we were crazy to be doing this job. I mean, he made it sound like that being a police officer meant certain death. The risk is very calculated. So just how dangerous is police work? Generally, policing isn't among the top ten most dangerous professions, falling well behind logging, fishing, driving a cab, trash collecting, farming, and truck driving. I don't point this out to diminish the tragedy of officers killed on the job. My point is that there are more dangerous jobs.

But I digress. Tonight, I want to salute the members of class 211.

I worked at Police headquarters for a month when I was first hired, and had the privilege of working with 5 of the sharpest people I've ever met; Chesnard, Hensell, Holden, Harding, and last but definitely not least Recruit Sergeant Thigpen. By the way, he's the only guy in the class I ever call by his first name. That's because of his age and wisdom. Yes, we had our own built-in old timer in our class. Kevin Thigpen was formerly an Atlanta police officer for about 5 years. He gave up the good life to become a professional football player, model, astronaut, marine biologist, and racecar driver for about 7 years. Then he decided he'd rather police than do all those other worthy things; so he came back. See how great this job is?

I soon discovered that these five guys were not the exception. Let me give you some examples:

Jones almost got kicked out of the academy for being hard on himself. Let me explain, most of us roll our eyes at others as if to say, "Forget you." Or "you're crazy." But Jones rolls his eyes at everything! I mean, his eyes are the portals to his soul. Well, we're in class and I think he was having problems grasping some Spanish and he rolled his eyes at the wrong time. He got in big trouble, got kicked out to the hall, but we all just looked at each other as if to say, Jones disrespectful? No way! Jones rolls his eyes all the time. For the next 8 weeks he didn't roll his eyes. That's discipline. He's rolled his eyes 47 times tonight...he don't mean nothin' by it.

Speaking of Spanish, we had one guy in the class who was one of the quietest people in the class, Lopez. But he became a star in our eyes, not because he spoke Spanish, but because he played the role of Spanish speaking suspects so well and really helped us learn how to use our Spanish to get the job done.

Another quiet guy was Martin. You've heard, "Quiet waters run deep?" Well, this guy is deep. Then there's the strong silent type, Thompson. I was behind Thompson at the shooting range for almost every event.

He would just stand there before he shot, with his hands clasped in front of him, chin down, and just stare at the target. When shooting started I think his concentration was so great that holes just appeared on the target magically. Then, when the smoke cleared, he'd be back in that stance, hands clasped, head down, holes all center mass, and a sly grin on his face.

It wasn't all work at the academy: There's Sauce, who taught us how to cook, AND how to say sauce. Heflin was my barometer of how the class was doing; if he was happy, we were fine, if he was sad (which was rare), we were in trouble, and if he was quiet...well, that never happened. Really, Heflin truly has the gift of helping others. He and several people in the class--Bautsch being the ringleader--were always quick to jump up and lend a hand. Garbutt went to all the remedial physical training, not because he needed it, but to encourage those of us who were required to go. Did I say "us?" I meant those poor other souls who were required to attend (I was required to be in the remedial training). That's one thing that will always stand out to me about this group of people, they almost always, as individuals, and as a group, went the extra mile to help each other. As the saying goes, "You never stand so tall as when you stoop to help someone." Even the Lord said the highest calling is to be called a servant.

On one occasion, early in the academy, I was telling a visiting instructor how impressed I was with the caliber of the students in our class--I'm not tooting my own horn, but I've been around the block...several times. Anyway, I was telling this instructor that the people in this class are on a par with any group I've ever worked with. After I said that someone shouted, "we love you too, Duke." And several people laughed. And it dawned on me: these young people are not only sharp, they don't even know how sharp they are. Like the line in the movie Swingers, "They're so money they don't know how money they are!" And that speaks to their upbringing. These guys were raised by people (parents, grandparents, step-parents, teachers, mentors) who expected hard work, academic excellence, and right living. And that is a testament to those here who had a hand in raising this fine group. I will always hold these guys dear to my heart because they are the epitome of what we look for in others, and especially in officers of the APD. I confidently entrust them with my life, and the people of Atlanta should be proud to have this group on the street protecting their lives and property.

I will conclude this dissertation with my answer to the last question posed in an assignment we had during our last week in the academy—can you believe it? An assignment during the last week of the academy? That's like giving homework on Friday! Anyway, the question was: "What would you do if faced with a situation and discover that you might not be a sheepdog?" Fortunately, class 211 has had a chance to find that answer through personal experience. We have known triumph and defeat, weakness and strength, and learned that the way of courage is always the right way. Class 211 knows it's ready because we have been fighting the wolves since we were young. We don't always do the right thing and we've been

knocked down, but none of us who made it through have ever been knocked out. A well-trained sheepdog will always give his best when able, and now, after our life experiences, capped off by attending the Atlanta Police Academy, we are not only sheepdogs, we're well-trained sheepdogs. Through an attitude of service before self, an attitude of excellence in all we do, a body ready to fight and defeat the wolf, and a solid rock of integrity holding us up, we will always remain sheepdogs. Class 211, I salute you (salute rendered). You're so money, you don't know how money you are.

I'm not going to say much else about the academy because, frankly, I don't remember a whole lot. It was fun, horrid, hard, easy, gratifying, confusing, painful, and overall a pain in the ass. But it prepared me about as well as you can be prepared for life as a police officer. After 6 months of the academy I was sworn-in on April 26, 2010, and sent to Field Training for the next three months.

In the Air Force, things were fairly well compartmentalized--I learned to be an officer at Officer Training School, then went to a year of flight school, then to survival school and advanced training, then I was a copilot, pilot, instructor pilot, evaluator pilot, staff officer, commander, and so on. The military was very regimented and gradual.

In contrast, the police academy was a fire hose and you had to drink as much as you could as fast as you could. In the morning you'd be in the classroom, and in the afternoon, you'd be wrestling in the dirt or doing pushups in the parking lot. One day you'd be running, and the next day you'd be in a patrol car driving an obstacle course. The challenges seemed to never stop in the academy. And then, when you thought you had made it, someone would spray you with pepper spray. As weird as this may sound, the unpredictability of the academy is really the only way to prepare someone for life on the street, because that's what life is like as a patrol officer, unpredictable and sometimes violent.

Excerpts from Field Training Diary

5/1/2010: Today is my first day on the job (field training) after being sworn in as an Atlanta Police Officer. Graduation is not officially until the end of July. It's a matter of no little pride that I am turning 52 years old this month and was still able to make it through the academy. Now, I have 12 weeks of field training in front of me.

My Field Training Officer (FTO) for the first 2 weeks is FTO Jesse Barmettler. He's been on the force for 5 years, and it looks like we'll get along well. He went to high school for a while in Germany, so his German is pretty good. We had about fifteen 911 calls.

We detained 4 people for suspected burglary because they matched the descriptions to a T. They had no evidence on them and denied any wrongdoing; however, the 3 boys had warrants and the girl was a runaway.

When we got out of the car, I hadn't heard Barmettler's call to Dispatch to check on warrants, but I knew as soon as he got out of the car and made a slight sidestep to the left of the biggest suspect, that he was going to arrest him. He had to be cool, because this guy gave all the signs of running--he hitched up his sagging pants and was looking around for an escape route. So I got the perp's (perpetrator) attention by complimenting him on the tattoos on his arm. I acted like I was impressed, and he held up his left arm to better show me the tat. When I grabbed his wrist, to feign admiration, my partner grabbed the other hand. We had him in cuffs in about 2 seconds. We hooked the others up with no problem.

Later, Barmettler asked how I knew he was going to arrest the guy. I couldn't explain it completely, except that his sidestep was not natural, and I somehow knew he was positioning himself to put cuffs on the guy. It was a gut feeling.

Funny thing, the girl was 15, but she sucked her thumb like a baby most of the time and didn't seem to care that anyone would find that strange. I guess she didn't have a parent who would make her stop when she was a toddler.

5/4: After 2 days off, this is my second day on the job. I'm in Zone 4 for two weeks on day shift. It is a very busy area; the busiest zone in the city. My supervisors, Sergeant King and

Lieutenant Kreher, are excellent. I hope the rest of the guys appreciate their good leadership. We answered about 20 calls, but most of them were over by the time we got there. It was a fun day, but I'm too tired to remember much of it. We helped arrest a drug dealer; drove right up on him in the act. I get to drive tomorrow.

5/5: I loved driving the patrol car. We arrested a woman who had attacked her husband with an 8-inch kitchen knife. She was drunk and mentally ill. We spent about 3 hours processing her at the hospital lockup and taking the knife to City Property. Of all the jobs I've had in my life-- laborer, truck driver, fast food, pilot and entrepreneur--the job that was the best schooling for this job was working in a mental health hospital when I was in college. (I was basically one of the guys in a white coat who handles the mental patients.) Many of the perps we run into are mentally ill, and having seen it before helps me recognize the symptoms now.

5/10: I saw another teenage (13-year-old) thumb sucking girl. Weird.

5/20: We went to a domestic dispute in a small apartment in the hood. The woman was acting as if the guy was totally at fault, but the guy had scratch marks on his face and neck. He said they were from his girl, so we knew she was going to jail for Battery. The weird thing was, we would have probably left him except he was so emotional, loud, and downright out of control that we couldn't just let him go without further investigation.

We found that the girl had a cut on the inside of her lip that she said came from him. As we were investigating, he stood up and hiked up his saggy pants, so I moved between him and the door. You could tell by his expression that I ruined his plans--he sat back down. He was so boisterous with two cops present, I had little doubt as to how violent he would be without us there. We asked him to settle down several times but he just couldn't control himself. (I know now that he was probably high on crack, but at the time I just thought he was stupid.)

5/25: I have a new trainer for two days, because my regular trainer had to take leave. My new FTO, Officer Harsch (not his real name), is a retired Marine. Let me explain: I think Marines are very unique (or at least many of them are). "Once a Marine, always a Marine," is not just a motto. They tend to be guarded in how they interact with people, even after they've been out of the service for many years. They're likeable, sociable, talkative, competent, and they think they're always right. This guy was no exception. He gave me talks of what a big guy he was in the Corps. He told me he retired as a Sergeant Major, the highest enlisted rank. I didn't want to tell him I retired as a Lt. Col, but he asked. After that, he insisted on calling me "Sir" and basically said policing was beneath me. He also insisted on catering to me by doing the reports, even though in the police force he outranked me. Oh well, he's a Marine and he means well.

We caught a 20-year-old with warrants for burglary and aggravated assault. He answered the door and when we said, "Are you Terrance?" he said yes. So we cuffed him before he even realized what had happened to him. Once we got him in cuffs, he got very loud, abusive and belligerent, screaming that he would kick out the windows of the squad car if we put him in it. We called for the paddy wagon, but two huge detectives showed up, put ankle cuffs on Terrance and put him in the back of their unmarked car. One of the detectives got in the back of the car with him.

I heard what sounded like Terrance banging on the window a few times, but then it stopped. I dare say the big detective in the back put an end to his shenanigans.

Terrance's mom was on scene, and she was as loud as her son, taking all our names and swearing she would have all our badges for violating her son's rights. (I'm starting to see a pattern among the thugs in the hood--many of them are very emotionally immature, and have very bad impulse control. Many just can't control themselves even when facing dire consequences, like jail.)

We went to a call where a young couple had called to say a man had been beaten up and was injured. When we got there, we found out the man was from a home for the mentally ill, located next to the restaurant the couple was going to. The lady was incensed that the workers in the home did not call an ambulance for the man.

The staff tried to explain that the man was faking his injuries and that no one had beat him up, that he was as crazy as a bed-bug. But the couple insisted on police and wanted us to go to the mental home and make them take the guy to the hospital. We went over to the home and, just as expected, he was a crazy old man. We thanked the couple for their concern. I guess they'd never met a crazy person before.

5/30: I started my field training with DUI Task Force, Night Watch. My trainer, Officer Castro, is a very laid-back guy, but he has a very intense job. We sit on the side of the highway and run radar looking for speeders which leads us to drunks. Had a fight on my very first stop. We've caught only 2 drunks in 5 days. But we give about ten speeding tickets a night. We've had people tell us they know a cop or give to the Fraternal Order of Police, trying to get out of a ticket. It doesn't work. Also, we've pulled over two cops and an EMT for speeding, and we've let them go with a warning. Of course, had they been drunk, we would have arrested them. We also pulled over a car that Andrew Jones, the baseball player, was a passenger in. He was cool, and the driver was sober.

6/9: Started training in Zone 2 a few days ago. This is the zone I hope to work in after my training and foot beat days are over (probably October). My new trainer, Senior Patrol Officer (SPO) Yankovich (not his real name), is weird. First, he's as wide as he is tall. He's about 5'06" and weighs about 300 pounds. A lot of it is muscle, but most of it is not. He's very quiet, and when he does talk, he's a low-talker (talks softly). After the first roll-call, SPO Yankovich didn't say anything to me, and I just followed him, thinking he'd tell me something. He walked into one of the back rooms, and I waited down the hall, thinking he was going to see someone. After about 5 minutes—which felt like 55—I snuck down the hall and saw him just sitting alone at a table. He didn't say anything to me when he came out about 10 minutes later.

We picked up a drunk who was stumbling down the sidewalk and gave him a ride home. He said he owned Kramer's, a very popular bar in town. We were skeptical until we dropped him at his apartment building; it was very nice. I turned to SPO Yankovich and said, "I think I saw this on an episode of Mayberry RFD." SPO Yankovich didn't even smile.

6/15: It's been a rough week, but I'm finally starting to break the ice with this FTO. He's having a rough time with our shift commander, Sergeant Willow (not her real name). The basic problem is that both of them are very stubborn, principled, and opinionated, so they rub each other the wrong way. Anyway, he looks to me for support, so at least we have something to interact about. We had a DUI arrest tonight.

6/16: We arrested a guy involved in an accident. He was so drunk, he couldn't even keep his balance to begin a field sobriety test. He blew 0.259 grams. The illegal limit is 0.08, so he was more than three times over the limit. What makes this hit home is that there was a fatality on the other side of town; a drunk who registered 0.231 grams ran a red light and struck a car, killing one person. This is an example of why it's important to get drunks off the street.

Going Swimming

One night during field training, my FTO and I found ourselves second in a car chase of a suspected carjacker. The chase went on at high speeds through a semi-residential area for about five minutes until the suspect ran smack-dab into a utility pole. I thought the chase was over, but the suspect bounded off into the woods. Being a "Trainee," there was no question; I was off on the chase. Another trainee from my class had been in the lead car, and the two of us were fast on the suspect's trail. We were so close, we could see the leaves of the bushes shaking in front of us as the suspect passed. Suddenly, we broke through the tree line and saw that the suspect had jumped into some water. Again, we were trainees so there was only one course of action for us; we jumped in after the suspect.

We caught up to the suspect as he tried to crawl out from the far bank, and the fight was reminiscent of something on a television show. It reminded me of the old TV show, Mutual of Omaha's Wild Kingdom, where "Jim" would always end up wrestling with a python. We fought to keep hold of the suspect while he tried to drown us. All of us were completely immersed in water several times before we were able to subdue the guy.

It was a struggle getting our cuffed suspect up the muddy slope. We considered taking his cuffs off or cuffing him in front so it would be easier, but quickly nixed that idea because the suspect was madder than a hornet. Once on the bank, we realized that the water was nothing more than a muddy ditch. Recent rains had raised the level of water to about five feet. We were covered from head to toe in muddy water.

That was my last call for the night because it took four hours to clean up and dry out.

Shooting a Bird

During field training, my FTO and I were responding with several other units to a fleeing burglar. After a short car chase, ending when the burglar wrecked his car, I joined the foot chase and found myself running right behind a fellow academy classmate, I'll call "Rusty." As we ran through the woods, we got word that the suspect was armed with a pistol and had a felony warrant.

Rusty and I knew the burglar had a decent head start; we had seen him jump from his wrecked car, so we kept up a good pace as we ran through the dark woods and tried to see our way with flashlights. Suddenly, as we were approaching a fallen tree, we heard a loud and agonizing scream. We both came to a stop.

"What in the world was that?" I asked in a hushed tone, as Rusty and I made eye contact to bolster our courage.

"I, uh, I don't know. But whatever it was, it wasn't good," Rusty answered, shining his light to see if he could see anything.

"It came from right in front of us," I said.

We could hear other units moving through the woods on either side of us, so we started forward, this time at a brisk walk and with our guns drawn, Rusty leading the way down a narrow path.

Suddenly, we heard another loud scream, or screech, and I saw a flash of light in front of Rusty's face, accompanied by a loud bang. I immediately got low to the ground, and right at that moment a huge owl flew directly over Rusty and then zoomed upward as it approached me. I noticed that Rusty was just standing there, and then I heard him yell, "Damn!" and then mumble something else.

"What?" I asked.

"I shot at a damn bird!" he yelled as his arms fell to his sides and his shoulders heaved.

The sounds of other officers approaching grew closer as I got on the radio to announce we were okay.

I could hear Rusty cursing to himself and sobbing as I went to help him get composed. But there was no consoling him.

"That's the third time I f@#*'d-up with this damn gun!" he said. I later learned that he had shot a dog the week before, and that earlier in training he had an inadvertent discharge when he fell during a chase.

I don't remember if anybody caught up to the suspect. I do remember that Rusty had to get some remedial training. However, he eventually made it through field training.

Fit for the Job

On my first night of Field Training with the DUI Task Force, my Field Training Officer (FTO), Officer Castro, and I were enroute to our beat when we saw another DUI Task Force officer, Officer Tequila (not his real name), on the side of the highway, conducting a field sobriety test. We pulled in behind Tequila's car, just in case he needed our help. The stop seemed to be going as planned until Tequila tried to handcuff the suspected drunk driver. That's when the driver decided he wasn't going to jail. As the driver started to swing, I grabbed his shoulders in mid swing and threw him on the ground. Castro and Tequila helped me subdue him, and it was all over in a matter of seconds.

We stood up from the scrum, and Tequila took custody of the driver. Tequila and Castro talked privately for a few minutes as I walked back to the patrol car, and then Castro and I proceeded down the interstate.

Castro didn't say anything about the fight so I just sat, hiding the abrasions on my hands and wondering if I was bleeding from the side of the head. At the same time, I was thinking, "Did I do the right thing? Was I supposed to jump on the driver that fast?" Castro continued to drive without commenting on the fight. For the remainder of the shift,

Castro never mentioned the fight. However, I thought about it a lot and finally came to the conclusion that I probably had acted hastily.

When we got back to the precinct, I saw Tequila talking to the sergeant and as I approached, I thought, "Here we go, I'm in trouble." However, as I got closer to the pair, the sergeant stood up and walked towards me smiling, saying, "I hear you did a good job tonight. Way to go." I was relieved, and both Tequila and Castro smiled and echoed the sergeant's sentiment.

As I was driving home, I realized I probably had a good temperament for this job. Over the next few weeks, I learned that acting before the suspect has a chance to do any damage is pretty much the ideal way to do the job. Of course, you have to wait until a crime occurs, or is about to occur, but if you are using "reasonable" reactions you can act. There's a lot more to it than that, but this night was a good lesson.

The next day I found out the driver, Mr. Rodriguez, had a blood alcohol level of .185 (over twice the illegal limit of .080), and he was armed with a bowie knife. Just saying.

A lot of the people I talk to, who aren't in law enforcement, have a story to tell about how they were treated poorly by law enforcement, usually during traffic stops. I can fully understand why they feel that way. However, what many people don't realize is how quick a seemingly innocent encounter can go bad. If you search "police encounters that go bad" on YouTube, you'll see many examples of police seemingly using excessive force on people, but the video usually doesn't show what led up to that force. In my experience, the force was necessary, because the suspect resisted in some way. Resisting arrest, even for a minor violation, will surely be met with some sort of force. That force may be a loud verbal command, the grabbing of an arm, or something as drastic as the officer pulling out his baton and hitting the suspect to gain compliance. That force can even be deadly if the officer thinks he's in danger of serious injury or death.

If commands don't work, and the officer doesn't use force, the only alternative an officer has is to let the person go. If officers started just letting people go when they resisted, there would be a lot more people resisting and a lot more criminals on the streets.

Here's the remedy for citizens: if a cop arrests you unlawfully, sue the crap out of them and the entity they work for--you won't be injured, the cop won't be injured, and the officer will learn a valuable lesson. The officer may even lose their job. Keep in mind that most law enforcement officers wear body cameras and most businesses and cities have cameras. If you're arrested unlawfully there will probably be sufficient evidence to support your claim.

During Tequila's DUI stop, the one I described above, the suspect seemed to be fully cooperating. He was drunk, but he wasn't acting crazy. In fact, he was very apologetic and seemed to be resigned to his fate. However, he exploded when he learned he was going to jail. If Castro and I hadn't been there, Officer Tequila would have had a huge fight on his hands, a fight in which he and the suspect would have both probably been injured or worse. So, officers have to always position themselves and be ready for the worst. Some officers can do this seemingly effortlessly. Others, not so much.

I usually could handle myself in such a way that I put citizens at ease. However, I was always sure to keep a safe distance between myself and a suspect, and even victims, during an encounter, in the event they tried to get physical. I learned early on to get handcuffs on people as soon as I had probable cause to arrest them.

If a citizen was standing too close to me, I'd take a step back. If they closed the gap, I'd step back again. I'd keep doing this until I ran out of room, at which time I would, in a polite way, say, "Excuse me, but could you not stand so close to me?" I'd go on to explain that I had a lot of weapons on my belt and, although they knew who I was (police officer), I didn't know who they were. Most people would understand, smile or apologize, and keep their distance (3-4 feet). But there were a few people who would take offense. These folks would usually voice their displeasure with something along the lines of, "Well, I've never been treated so rudely! Do you think I'm some sort of criminal?"

I'm sure a lot of these people told their family and friends about the rude officer they had met. In the post-COVID era, social distancing is not as unusual as it was when I was a cop.

I can remember during one nighttime traffic stop, the driver started telling jokes as I tried to tell her why I had stopped her. She was funny, but I didn't laugh, and I continued to explain the stop to her. She actually got upset that I wasn't laughing with her, saying, "You have no sense of humor." What this lady didn't realize was that I was standing outside of her car, on a busy city street, in a bad neighborhood, and her car registration showed the car owner as having a warrant for domestic battery. As it ended up, she had just bought the car and the previous owner was wanted. She got away with just a warning. However, before I found out who she was, I was going under the assumption that she was a criminal suspect. Frankly, I assumed that everyone I stopped was armed and dangerous. That doesn't mean I immediately cuffed them, but it did mean I was ready for anything.

Law enforcement officers come in contact with dozens of strangers every day under some stressful situations. Smart officers will treat people with respect, but they'll also stay on guard in the event this "victim" is really a "perp" or mentally unstable. Staying on guard is not always just a physical thing but also has a lot to do with how you talk to someone. When an officer asks that someone keep their hands out of their pockets, they have to do it so that the person has no question that the officer means business. To do otherwise could lead to a bad situation. Sure, you may think it rude when the officer says, "Don't put your hands in your pockets," or "Stay in the car," or "No, don't go into your glovebox," but they are doing it for a very good reason.

Chapter 2. You Can Run, But You Really Should Hide

Ram-shackled

Early one morning, during day shift, Officers Hernandez and Severance were dispatched to two suspicious males walking away from a house carrying a TV. In addition, there was an audible alarm at the house reported over the radio. Being the smart cops they are, Hernandez and Severance knew from the comments on Dispatch that the suspects were heading towards a creek behind the sub-division, so they started to that area. I overheard their radio call and responded to the house where the alarm was sounding.

When Hernandez and Severance arrived at the creek, they saw the two males walking on the dry creek bed, heading towards Sumter Street, but they no longer had the TV with them. The suspects ran when they saw Hernandez and Severance, and the officers saw one of the suspects throw a bag in the woods. Officer Edwards (not his real name), also monitoring the radio, responded to the location and was able to catch one of the thieves, Mr. Bell. However, the other thief got away.

Meanwhile, at the house, I found that a back window had been broken, and the house had been rummaged through. The victim arrived home during my investigation.

I found it funny that the victim kept saying her house had been "ram-shackled," instead of "ransacked" or "rummaged through." She said it so often that I started using the phrase (I find myself still using it on occasions—makes me smile).

A neighbor also showed up and said she had seen the suspects leaving the yard with the TV.

I drove the neighbor over to where Edwards was holding Mr. Bell. The neighbor confirmed that Mr. Bell was one of the men she saw leaving the victim's yard. In addition, the neighbor gave us a very good description of the other suspect. "He's about 5 feet, 10 inches tall with long dreads, blue jeans, black tennis shoes, and he was wearing a gray tee shirt under a green tee shirt."

Hernandez and Severance recovered the bag that Mr. Bell had thrown and discovered it contained a tablet computer and a knife, taken from the victim's home. The suspect denied that he stole a TV. In fact, he denied that he had anything to do with a burglary.

We had crime scene technicians process the scene, confirmed that a TV had been stolen, finished our reports, and were happy we had caught at least one of the suspects. Frankly, I didn't think we'd ever catch the other suspect.

That afternoon I was driving through a neighborhood, not far from the house that had been "ram-shackled," when I saw a guy wearing a baseball cap, black tennis shoes, jeans, and a gray shirt. As I got closer, I realized that the man had dreads pushed up under his cap. Up to this point I had forgotten about the suspect who got away earlier.

The guy was standing by the woods, looking around as if he wanted to make sure no one was watching him. I thought he might be looking to see if the coast was clear so he could take a pee on the side of the road.

I pulled right up to the man and before he had time to think I was out of my car, asking him questions. The guy started to sweat right away. His story about, 'Well...uh...I'm going to see a friend,' was not convincing.

The man was looking around as if to see if anyone else was in the area (a sign that he was either going to fight or flee), and just as he was hitching up his pants--which had been hanging below his butt cheeks--I grabbed him. A struggle ensued and, thanks to my top-notch academy defensive tactics training, and his exercise regime of smoking weed and watching TV, I quickly got the better of him.

Officer Edwards showed up as I was putting the suspect into my car.

"Dude, I've been looking for this guy all day!" Edwards said. "I knew he'd be wearing a gray shirt." Edwards explained that many semi-pro perps will wear two shirts so that they can commit their crime and then shed a shirt so that they don't match a witness's description.

Edwards looked towards the woods and said, "I wonder..."

Before finishing his sentence, he walked about 10 feet into the woods and came out holding a flat screen TV.

Edwards was all smiles, nodded his head towards the suspect and said, "Book him, Danno." (If you've never watched the TV show Hawaii Five-0, that reference won't mean anything to you. Google it.)

Shave and a Haircut

One afternoon I was dispatched to a shoplifter at a Dollar Store on my beat. The store manager, Ms. Bernard, told me that a man, later identified as Mr. Brown, just shoplifted from her store.

I had met Ms. Bernard a few months prior when the store first opened. At that time, I had thought of her as just a complainer—every time I saw her, she'd complain about something that a homeless person had done, or tell me, after the fact, about a shoplifter. It got to the point that I avoided her, not even driving through the Dollar Store parking lot for fear she'd flag me down with another complaint that was too general or too old to investigate. Over time, I realized she was under siege by the many homeless, mentally ill, impulsive juveniles, or just plain bad people who thought that everything in the Dollar Store was theirs for the taking. My heart went out to her and her situation and I started coming to the store almost every day if I had the time. I learned to appreciate the stress she was under. This Dollar Store was new, and the only one within five miles. If the thieves managed to put this store out of business, the people of this poor neighborhood wouldn't have a local store.

"What does he look like?" I asked.

"He's kind of tall, and he ain't got no front teeth. He ain't homeless, he lives up around the corner. He's got on black pants, and he's wearing a big puffy black jacket," she answered.

It wasn't a particularly cold day, in the upper 60's, and I was trying to visualize a man with a 'big puffy jacket' walking around the neighborhood. The thought of the Puffy Shirt episode of Seinfeld crossed my mind, and I made an inappropriate laugh.

"Yeah, the jacket has big, like, bubbles in it, like a Michelin Man," she added. "He came in, walked around a little, then went over to the cigarette lighters and jammed several packs of them in his jacket and down his pants. I was sort of watching him and when the security beepers at the front door went off, I was right there."

"Did he get outside the store with the lighters?" I asked.

"He was right outside the door when I caught up to him. When I asked him about the lighters, he acted all innocent, and stuff, but after, like, talking to him he removed a few packs from his jacket and some fell on the floor. When I went to pick them up, he just ran away. He's a big man so I couldn't stop him. You've got to do something, Officer Duke, this guy's been robbing me blind for the past two months. He ran out of here just minutes before you got here. I've got video, you want to see it?"

The video was very clear, Dollar Store has a great high definition system, and on it I could see that everything had happened just as Ms. Bernard said. But there was more.

Not only did Dollar Store have cameras on the inside, they had several cameras on the outside of the store, with great views of the parking lots and other businesses near the intersection. On one camera we could clearly see the suspect leave the store and jog over to the barbershop across the street.

"This guy has been robbing me blind for the past two months, but this is the first time I've caught him in the act." she said.

I followed the route the suspect had taken, about a fifty- yard jog, and went into the barbershop. I was greeted by several people, many of whom I knew from the neighborhood, and, sure enough, Mr. Brown was in the barber chair with a big toothless smile, as if he was greeting a good friend. He was getting his hair cut and neck shaved.

"Sir, is this your jacket?" I asked, as I walked to where it was lying next to a wall on the other side of the barber chair.

He hesitated, but then said, "Yeah, it's a little too warm for a jacket in here."

I agreed, saying, "Yes sir, it's warm, but this makes a great place to hide stuff you shoplift from the store." I picked up the jacket and as I did so a couple of packages of Bic lighters fell to the floor.

Mr. Brown just shrugged his shoulders, and with a weak smile, said, "I guess you got me."

I considered calling for another unit to come pick us up at the barbershop but decided against it knowing it would take several minutes for one to arrive, and I could walk him over in half the time. I walked Mr. Brown, in cuffs, back over the fifty-yard trek, in what some people would refer to as a "Perp Walk."

A lot of onlookers stood in the parking lot and in front of the stores, and Mr. Brown adamantly protested his arrest as "harassment" and "racist," trying to draw sympathy from the crowd. "Anyway, this is just petty s--t. I'll be out of jail before you get off your shift!" he shouted.

His protests got louder as we neared the patrol car, and I had some issues getting him into the back seat.

Although we did have car cameras (this was before the days of body cameras in the Department), my car camera was off. Mr. Brown's protests and insults reached a crescendo and I'm sure that a few people wondered if I was beating or abusing him. "Well, at least I've got the Dollar Store cameras covering me," I thought.

In the back seat, Mr. Brown continued to call me everything but a Child of God, and let me know I was wasting my time prosecuting such a minor offense. But I had a surprise for Mr. Brown.

"How many times do you think Mr. Brown has stolen from the store?" I asked, as Ms. Bernard stood outside my driver's window.

"I don't know," she began, and after a short pause, said, "But he comes into the store almost every day, and I'm sure he takes something on most days!" she said.

"So, you guys have been open for about six months. How long has he been coming into the store?"

"Oh, for at least two months. Probably longer."

"So, conservatively, he's stolen from you about thirty times?"

"Yeah, yeah, that'd be a conservative number," she answered. "But I can get the guys at I-Verify to check for me?"

"I-Verify, what's that?"

"That's the system that controls our cameras, they're up in New York, or somewhere, and they monitor, record and control all our cameras."

After explaining my case to a Zone-2 Investigator, I was able to get them to come out to the store. By checking with I-Verify, within minutes they confirmed over a dozen cases of shoplifting by Mr. Brown in the past week. Habitual Shoplifting is a felony in Georgia, so Mr. Brown didn't make it back home by the end of my shift. In fact, I found out, months later, that he had been implicated in hundreds of shoplifting cases. Last I heard, Mr. Brown was still in jail.

From that time on I was Ms. Bernard's hero. She greeted me like her BFF every time I came into the store. In addition, we made several more cases, with the help of I-Verify, and although Ms. Bernard is no longer working at that Dollar Store, the store is still open and appears to be thriving as I write this seven years later. This would have never happened without Mr. Brown needing a shave and a haircut.

Damaged Caddy

On a hot July day, I was dispatched to a car vandalism. Dispatch advised me that the victim said someone had been sitting on his vehicle and the vehicle was now damaged. As I parked and walked up to the address, I could clearly see damage to the top, sides, and lock of the trunk on an older model, but nicely kept, Cadillac.

As I assessed the damage, an older, distinguished looking man approached me from the house, using a cane to help him keep his balance.

"I was visiting an old friend and I looked out the window and saw a young punk sitting on my trunk and listening to his headphones," he began. "I came to the porch and yelled, 'Hey you, get off my car!' and he hopped down. He walked away so I didn't think any more about it until, after five to ten minutes, I came back out and saw all this damage!"

"I mean, look, officer, he has totally ruined up my paint job! Now, who does that type of s#!t!" he said in disgust. "I wasn't about to follow him 'cause I'm old."

"It appears that he was trying to get into the trunk. He sure did make a mess of it, but at least he didn't steal anything. How long ago did all this happen?" I asked.

"Oh, no more than fifteen minutes ago," he said.

The victim proceeded to give me a good description of the suspect. After getting all his information, I had the victim fill out a written statement. I put out a BOLO (Be on the lookout) on the suspect over Dispatch, so other units could help me search the area. The investigation took over an hour because I had to wait on Crime Scene Unit photographers.

"I definitely will prosecute this--that asshole caused me thousand's in damage," the victim said as I was leaving.

Within a few blocks of driving, I saw someone who fit the suspect's description to a T, standing in a convenience store parking lot. I swung my patrol car onto the lot, and as I approached, I saw that the suspect had several objects in the pockets of his pants. He acted nonchalant, as if he hadn't seen me (though I'm sure he had), and the first thing I said to him was, "Put your hands behind your back." I had the cuffs on him before he had time to protest.

In his pant pockets I found two screwdrivers, a spark plug, and a small amount of marijuana. Also, he had a prybar stuffed down his pants, kept in place by tying it to a belt loop.

Spark plugs and screwdrivers are often used to break car windows, and pry-bars have many purposes--busting locks and opening compartments to name a few. Weed? That's what they buy with the money they make from breaking into cars. From all appearances this guy was a self-contained, fully equipped, Theft-From-Auto Shop.

The victim came by and confirmed that I had the right person. It was towards the end of the shift and I was hoping to avoid taking the suspect to jail (just scratch a citation for the weed) by getting him and the victim to come to some sort of agreement, but that wasn't to be; Dispatch advised me that the suspect had two active warrants for breaking into cars.

Another officer came by and I asked him to take the suspect's tools to City Property while I started processing him for jail. "Forget property, this stuff is evidence," the other officer said. He went on to explain how I could charge the suspect with Possessing Tools of the Crime (Entering Auto). I charged him with four different "Tools of the Crime" charges, in addition to the weed and Criminal Damage to Property.

I never got called into court for the case, but at least the victim got some satisfaction. In addition, the amount of car break-ins in the area went noticeably down for the next few weeks.

Being a police officer is very satisfying work, made a lot easier when the suspects think the coast is clear. Warning to perps: the coast is never clear; we're always looking for you.

Dirty Old Man

One day I was dispatched to a suspicious person on school property. Dispatch said he was riding a bike and enticing children on the playground. The caller gave a description of a black male wearing dark clothing with a gray beard and gray hair.

I didn't see anybody that fit the description at the school and was told the suspect had left the scene. I talked with several teachers and they said the suspect had been seen at the school before, but always left whenever approached by an adult. This time, the kids had told the teachers about the man wanting to give them candy and soda, so they called the police.

I didn't take long at the school because I was hopeful I could catch up to the suspect. I put out an updated BOLO for him as I left the school.

Just down the block I saw a man with dark clothes, a salt-and-pepper beard, and a partially gray head of hair. He was sitting on a bike at the Shell gas station and I asked him where he had come from.

"I just came from Grady (Hospital)," he said.

"Were you anywhere near the elementary school?"

"Nah, man. I don't go that way," he said, waving his hand and making a face as if to say, "Are you crazy?"

I called the school principal, and she came by the gas station and confirmed that my suspect was the same man who had ridden through the playground and asked children if they would come with him, promising them candy and soda.

Due to the fact there were children and possible sex crimes involved, I got the Crimes Against Children Unit to come on scene.

I don't think I could ever work sex crimes against children on a regular basis. I feel the penalty for anyone who sexually abuses a small child should be death, or at least a life sentence in prison. It would be very frustrating to work a child's case, even if you make a great case, and see the perpetrator walk away with just a few years in prison. In addition, I think seeing these cases over a prolonged period would do something to your psyche—PTSD must be prevalent with children's sex crime investigators.

The result of our work was several charges for the suspect and increased safety for the children. I later learned the suspect had a prior arrest for Cruelty to Children and Aggravated Sodomy.

Thank God, the suspect didn't keep on riding his bike away from the area.

Piss Test

My Trainee and I were dispatched in reference to a person urinating in public at the CVS Pharmacy. Upon arrival, the manager, Mr. Davis, said he saw a black male with baggy pants and a tan coat urinating against the wall just outside the front door of his store. He showed us where the man had urinated right outside the door. The urine was still steaming and streaming across the sidewalk. I asked my Trainee to check if the urine was still warm, but he refused. Smart guy.

Mr. Davis said he told the male to leave immediately and that he was calling police. Mr. Davis said he could identify the male if he saw him again.

As we canvassed the immediate area, we found the suspect sitting at a MARTA bus stop, thirty yards away from the store, on the other side of the parking lot.

Great hiding place; a see-through plexiglass bus stop.

Some criminals just don't know when it's time to run. I don't know if it's stupidity, laziness, contempt for law enforcement, or just old-fashioned bravado; many criminals think they can commit crimes with impunity and never get caught. I'm going to take an educated guess and say many of them probably were never appropriately corrected by their parents when they were younger; they'd lie and get away with it, use violence and get away with it, stay out all night with no repercussions, and basically rebel against their parents and society without paying a price. So, they think the same rules apply when they're older. Or maybe they're depressed and just don't care. I've had many juveniles and young people tell me they didn't care if they lived or died; they just live for today. Who's to say?

Chapter 3. Excerpts from Morning Watch Diary

1/23/2011. I arrested a guy for driving without a license and then found out he gave me a wrong name and date-of-birth (DOB). Once I had the real name, I found out his license was suspended. So I arrested him for driving with a suspended license and for giving a false name and DOB to a police officer. Found a gun in his car as well. He asked me if I'd made any real arrests that night, and I told him he IS a real arrest. He initially gave me his brother-in-law's name and DOB; I call that a real crime. Someone who would abuse the trust of a friend or relative is just not worthy of mercy from the court. He could have caused his brother-in-law some real hardship.

Had problems with Sergeant Willow (not her real name), the same shift sergeant that was bothering my first FTO, Officer Yankovich. Sergeant Willow embarrasses people on the radio almost every night and she's way too abrasive. She doesn't know how to correct people; she only knows how to scold. She lied twice about what I'd said and done during a traffic stop. I let her know she wasn't at the scene and only knew what she knew from radio calls. Earlier in the night she had tried to get me to take a car that had a broken driver's seatbelt; sorry, I'm not doing that. She was incredulous when I told her I actually wear my seatbelt. I thought about taking the car with the bad belt, but the old saying, "Crap rolls downhill," came to mind, and I decided to turn the car in. Sergeant Willow giving me permission to take the car without a seat belt would not cover me in the event I got in a crash without my belt on. So that didn't put me in good graces with her. Later in the night, I called for an extra car using the phrase "5-9 (Officer Needs Assistance), NOT right away," which means don't hurry, just one more person when you can make it. Sergeant Willow said I said "5-9, right away" which means I wanted someone immediately. I told her to listen to the tapes. I know what I said because those two things are quite different. She wouldn't listen, and then said that she wasn't mad at me until I argued with her about the last thing. I told her that wasn't true, because she had already yelled at me on the radio and the phone before we ever got together to "discuss" the incident. She doesn't have a good reputation on the Watch; a guy who's known her for years said she's only been on the street for about a year--spent the rest of her career in an office.

1/28/11. We got a new Lieutenant, Lieutenant Compost (not his real name), last night. Not impressed. He reminds me of Sergeant Willow; no sense of humor, always covering her own butt, and continually looking to criticize others. Good leaders use their sense of humor to help people through the learning process, keep communication open, and get through tough times. And good leaders look to help their people, not themselves. I hope I'm wrong. The Lieutenant said he'd heard good things about me, and he wants me to apply for the Traffic Car in Zone-2. I'd love it, but I doubt I'll get it. That job is for the most experienced officers.

Chapter 4. Signal-24

Running with Scissors

I went to an unusual vandalism call at a nice home in the Buckhead community of Atlanta. An attractive middle-aged woman answered the door and invited me in.

"Officer, I took this dress out of the washing machine, only to discover that the hem was ripped out in two places," she said, as she held up a lightweight sun-dress and showed me the damage. I noted that, indeed, the hem of the dress had two places where the stitching in the hem had come loose. Neither area was longer than a couple of inches.

I pretended to write something in my notepad, while at the same time wondering how I was going to put this information into a report.

The lady began walking towards another part of the house, as I followed, saying, "And look here, officer, the sheets on this bed have been deliberately damaged." The lady pulled back the blanket on a large oak bed, revealing several circles and hearts, drawn with magic marker, on the underlying sheet.

"Officer, I marked the damaged areas with a marker so you can see that this sheet has several areas that have been deliberately damaged. Look here," she continued, "see these raised areas? You can tell this is deliberate because the raised bumps are in a straight line."

I had to look closely to see what she was referring too, and I saw that there were some "puckered" places on the sheet. I was tempted to comment that the circles and hearts she drew around the damaged areas were worse than the damage itself.

"Ma'am, this looks like normal wear and tear to me."

"Well, these sheets weren't like this yesterday, and my dress wasn't ripped yesterday, either. And look at this, there's a scratch on this table." She showed me a 1-inch superficial scratch on the top of a bed-side table. Again, the scratch had been circled with a magic marker.

Using my best non-judgmental voice, I repeated myself, saying, "Ma'am, this really looks like normal wear and tear to me."

"You mean this end table?" she countered.

"I mean everything. Everything you've shown me so far appears to be normal wear."

Up to this point, despite her dubious examples of wanton destruction, she had been speaking in a normal voice that, despite the things she was saying, made her appear to be a stable adult. Now, her voiced raised as she made her case.

"Officer, you can't tell me that all this damage is normal! Come...come, look at what happened to my car," she said as she beckoned me towards a door.

In the driveway was a beautiful blue BMW sedan, a car that must have cost close to $100,000 dollars.

"Now, you're going to have to get low to see it," she continued as we moved towards the front of the vehicle. At this point she carefully got down on a knee and beckoned me to look under the front of the car.

I got down on one knee and looked to where she had been pointing under the grill. "I don't see anything," I said, as I pulled out my flashlight.

"No. You have to look lower," she said as she lowered herself on the driveway and pointed to the underside of the vehicle.

I had to lay on the driveway to see where she was pointing and noticed that the scratch guard under the front of the car had a few scratches. "Ma'am, it looks like your scratch guard has a few scratches but, again, that's normal."

She got louder and insisted that she didn't put those scratches there.

"Ma'am, it's normal for a scratch guard to get a few scratches. That's why it's called a 'scratch guard.'"

"It's not normal! I didn't put them there! Somebody is deliberately trying to sabotage me!" she said, raising her voice higher with each sentence.

As I was getting up from the driveway, I noticed a scratch above one of the headlights. "Ma'am, if we're going to report the scratches on the scratch guard, why don't we report this scratch above the light."

"Oh, I reported that last week," she replied.

I asked her who she thought might have caused the damage, who had access to her property, and several other questions. Her bottom line was, "I have no idea who caused this damage, all I know is that it appears to be purposeful and I didn't do it…and I want a police report!"

"Well, from what I've seen here it all looks like normal wear; nothing done intentional or out of the ordinary." I said. I just couldn't imagine how I could report this damage as a possible crime.

"Ma'am, I'm sorry, but this is not a crime," I said, then turned and walked towards my patrol car. I reported on the radio, "Dispatch, show me code-12 (Investigated, nothing to report), normal wear and tear." I was tempted to add "Code-24 (Demented Person)" but resisted the urge.

When I returned to the precinct at the end of my shift, I was surprised to find the lady standing by the front desk. I pulled aside the front desk officer.

"What is that lady doing here?"

The desk officer smiled, and said, "She came in about an hour ago, and she wants me to do a report on damage to some sheets. I tried to get out of it, but Sergeant said to do the report." Then she leaned towards me and said, in a hushed voice, "I think the woman's a little unstable."

"Really? Well, if we do that report, we're more unstable than she is," I responded. We both laughed and I went on my way.

I later learned that the desk officer did the report.

24 Knows 24

Responding to a domestic situation, I was greeted at the front door by a lady claiming that her 30-year old son hadn't come home until 6 o'clock that morning, and that he had been with a woman and smelled like alcohol. She went on to say that she thinks he works for the CIA or FBI and that he's up to something "fishy."

"Have you guys had a physical fight?" I asked.

"No, but we've been arguing and he refuses to get out of bed," the woman replied.

The woman was very distraught and went on to give me a laundry list of other problems with her son. She was what I refer to as a "professional talker," the kind of person who will talk non-stop, giving few chances to interrupt them. In addition, her rants were loaded with paranoid conspiracy theories.

After a few minutes I decided to get the son's side of story. The woman followed me as I walked towards the son's bedroom; I knew he was awake because there was no way anyone could sleep with the woman yelling. The bedroom door was open, but as I tried to make contact with the son, the woman continued to bombard me with all of her son's problems. At that point I heard my backup officer call from the front door.

I walked back to the front door and said, "Could you talk to this lady?"

He agreed to interview her, and as I walked back inside I whispered to him, "Be advised, 24-City."

The woman had apparently overheard me, and roared, "I am not crazy!"

She went on to read me the riot act, telling us that she used to be a police dispatcher and she knows what a "24" is. A supervisor came on scene and I don't know how I didn't wind up in Internal Affairs.

Stabbed by a Ghost

One evening I heard an officer dispatched to a Person Stabbed call, so I went to back the officer up. I was the first one on scene, and there was a male lying in the front yard of the house with a steak knife in his abdomen. The knife was sticking up in the air and the man was holding it, rolling side to side, and groaning, like you'd see in a movie. I called for an ambulance. There wasn't much, if any bleeding, so I left the knife where it was.

The man claimed that there was a knock on his door, and when he opened it a black male in a red hat (No, this was long before MAGA hats) and white t-Shirt stabbed him. He explained that the suspect went through his wallet and left.

As I was checking the man over, I found that his wallet was still in his back pocket. The man groaned as if he was in significant pain so I didn't press him for a further explanation.

The primary officer and the Grady Bus arrived. The man explained to the primary officer that the suspect ran down the street, in the direction from which I had come to the scene. I definitely had not seen anyone matching the description of the man anywhere near the location.

A lookout for the suspect was given to units in the area. Grady EMTs removed the knife from the man's abdomen and told us it had only entered about an inch into fat tissue and was not life threatening. An EMT pulled us aside and told us they had extensive experience with the victim, and he had a history of mental illness and had threatened suicide several times in the past.

We entered the house because the door was hanging open, and we wanted to make sure the suspect had not gone into the residence. The house was bare except for a mattress, chair and refrigerator. In the kitchen was a set of steak knives that matched the one the victim had been stabbed with.

Chapter 5. Strange Things

Arresting a Security Guard

When I got into my patrol car after roll-call, about 0630 hours, I realized that the gas gauge was on empty and the fuel-low warning light was on. I thought about calling a wrecker for some emergency fuel, but the Northside Drive fuel station was only 15 minutes away so I took the chance and hit the road.

It was still dark as I pulled into the fuel station, but I could see a man peeing on the cinder block wall that surrounded three sides of the property, in plain view, about 10 feet from the main street. I was in a hurry to get some gas and continued to the pumps about 150 yards away, behind a building. I noticed that there was no guard in the guard shack as I passed it. (Vandalism at City properties had prompted the hiring of private security guards throughout Atlanta, so a security guard was always on location.)

As I exited the station, I noticed there was still no guard in the guard shack and I could see the man, who'd been peeing on the wall, standing on the main road under a MARTA bus sign. I had a hunch that the man in question was, in fact, the security guard, but I stopped to talk with him and make sure.

As soon as I came to a stop, the man started walking away from me. He was about 6 feet, 3 inches tall, husky, and walking at a brisk pace. I called for him to stop but he just kept going. I hurried to catch up and in a louder voice yelled, "Police! Stop! I need to talk to you." The man continued walking and didn't look back.

I caught up to him and yelled for him to stop again, but he kept right on walking, ignoring me. I walked with him for about 20 paces and, in my best command voice, yelled, "Stop, or I'll pepper spray you!" The man immediately stopped and turned his body partially towards me.

"I don't have to talk to you," he said.

"Yes, you do. Why are you walking away? I need to talk to you."

The man rolled his eyes and explained again that he didn't have to talk to me. Fortunately, he didn't start walking again. I could tell that he was very wary of getting hit with pepper spray.

"Are you the security guard at the fuel station?" I asked.

The man rolled his eyes again and said he didn't have to talk to me.

"Well, if you don't start talking, I'm going to arrest you for urinating in public. Now, answer my question."

We continued to talk for the next 5 minutes, but the man continued to refuse answering questions. As I moved to place the man in handcuffs, he suddenly had a change of heart and admitted he was the security guard. He went on to explain that he was hoping to catch the 7:15 bus, so he had changed out of his security uniform and gone to the street. He said that he doesn't officially get off until 0730, but if he doesn't catch the 7:15 he has to wait until 8-O'Clock for a bus.

I asked to see his ID (for about the 5th time) but the man kept stonewalling me. I cuffed him.

The day shift security guard came on the scene and several APD officers dropped by. It was a slow Saturday morning and mine was the only case going on at the time. (If given the time, APD officers will always back each other up, even without being asked. Unfortunately, our call volume was so high we usually found ourselves alone, unless we asked for backup. The only time I rode with a partner was when I had a Trainee or during a special event.)

The man got tearful after I cuffed him, and he asked me to call his mother. He also begged me, over and over, to not arrest him.

"How old are you, Sir?" I asked.

He admitted that he was 26 years old, and I confirmed his identity when I found his ID card in his backpack.

Eventually, because the man was so upset, I agreed to call his mother for him.

"I knew his mouth would get him in trouble," was the first thing the mother said after I explained the situation to her. She went on to explain that she worked for the City of Atlanta and had gotten the job for her son as a favor from a friend. I felt sorry for Mom, but after what I had gone through with her son, I wasn't inclined to release him with just a citation--I let her know how to get her son from City Jail.

The man continued to sob in the back of my patrol car, and several officers joked about how "mean" I was. As I sat putting together paperwork for the jail, I thought about how immature this huge man in my back seat was; he had the emotional maturity of a 4th grader.

As I put the car in gear to head towards the jail, I noticed that the begging and crying had subsided. I looked in my rear-view mirror and noticed that the man was still awake but had found comfort by vigorously sucking his thumb.

This wasn't the first time I'd seen a full-grown adult suck their thumb. As a police officer I've run into several adults who suck their thumbs. Ask any big city cop and I'm sure they've seen the same thing.

About three years after this incident, I was at the Howell Mill Drive fuel station and thought I recognized a new security guard as the same thumb-sucker I had arrested years earlier. I was pretty sure he was the same guy. After seeing him off-and-on for a month, I pulled into the pumps one day and saw the man asleep, sucking his thumb in the guard booth. Yep, it was definitely the same guy.

I never saw him again after that.

Weed-Ass

One morning a Trainee and I were on routine patrol and stopped by a parking deck that had experienced a lot of car break-ins in the past few weeks. While patrolling through the deck, we came upon a parked white Lincoln Town Car, engine running, with two females sitting in the front seats. We walked up to the vehicle to ask them if they lived here or needed any help. The driver, Ms. Macklin, said that her girlfriend's sister lived there. The lady in the passenger seat, presumably the "girlfriend," showed us her parking pass for the complex.

"We just got into the car and were about to leave to bring my friend's son to school," Ms. Macklin said.

We noticed the child in the backseat appeared to be very young, about 3 or 4 years old, and he was sitting on pillows, without a car seat. As I walked to the rear of the vehicle to check the license plate, Ms. Macklin put the car in reverse and backed up about a foot, then put it in Drive and drove away as if nothing was amiss. We got into our patrol car and followed her out of the parking deck and performed a traffic stop on Huff Road.

When I asked Ms. Macklin for her license, she said, "I don't have my driver's license on me."

"Where is it at, Ma'am?"

"Well, I left it at home because I was only driving a little way."

"Ma'am, you really need to carry your license with you whenever you drive," I said, as I pulled out a notebook. "Give me your name and date of birth."

She gave me a first and last name and a birthdate. We checked her information on our car computer but didn't come back with any hits (data).

I went back to the Lincoln to verify her information.

"Ma'am, I'm not coming back with any person with a Georgia driver's license with that name and date of birth," I said.

"Oh! I have a Tennessee driver's license," she said, as if I was supposed to intuitively know that the first time I asked. "But, here, I've got a Georgia State identification card, if that will help."

I took her ID card and wasn't surprised in the least when, on my car computer, I discovered she had a suspended Tennessee license and no license in Georgia.

We placed her under arrest for driving on a suspended driver's license and for not having the child properly restrained.

We requested a female officer to search Ms. Macklin but were advised that there were none available. We had her empty out her pockets to make sure she didn't have any contraband on her. As we were placing her in the patrol car, I got a distinct odor of unburnt marijuana mixed with excrement. I know that's a weird combination, but to a cop that means only one thing; she had shoved weed up her butt.

When we questioned her about the weed smell, she assured us that they had smoked some earlier in the day but that she didn't have any weed on her now.

When we got to City Jail, I warned the female intake officer, Officer Anderson, of our suspicions. Sure enough, the suspect had an acute case of Weed-Ass. Well, there's another charge added to her case.

After this incident, Officer Anderson gave me the nickname, "Bloodhound."

Out of Jurisdiction

There was a gas station with a small convenience shop on my beat that had a serial shoplifter who stole from them several times a week for a period of several weeks. The thefts didn't always occur on my shift, but when they did I would respond as fast as I could, only to find the suspect had escaped through a trail in the woods (a trail in city woods is called a "cut" in police lingo) right behind the store. Unfortunately, the cut came out into a housing project outside the city limits of Atlanta; the cut came out in Cobb County, outside of my jurisdiction.

Police officers are allowed to chase and apprehend people in other jurisdictions as long as the crime occurs in their jurisdiction and the chase is continuous. Unfortunately, it was about a 10-minute drive to get to the other side of the cut so, unless I personally saw the perp go into the woods and I made chase, I was out of luck. The ten-minute drive was too circuitous to be considered "continuous." In addition, the cut took only about three minutes to run and opened up into a housing project. Even if I saw the perp and made chase, the odds of me catching him in that short time, and in that housing project, were slim.

One day I was in the parking lot of the gas station, and a patrol car from Cobb County Police Department came into the parking lot. I talked to the officer for a couple of minutes and found out he was the beat officer for the beat right next to mine. We exchanged pleasantries, and I told him about the shoplifter who used the cut and ran back into Cobb County to get away.

"The description you give sounds like a guy I've had run-ins with," the Cobb County officer said in response to my information.

Our jurisdictions didn't monitor each other's radios, so we exchanged phone numbers just in case we needed to get in touch.

Within five minutes after talking to the Cobb County officer, and only a minute or two after leaving the gas station parking lot, I got dispatched to a shoplifting call at that same gas station. I immediately called my new friend.

"Hey, that guy just hit the gas station," I said. "You think you can get to the end of that cut in a few minutes?"

"Dude, I'm already there," he answered. "I came over here just after talking to you."

I kept the Cobb County officer on the phone as I continued towards the gas station. Just as I reached the station, I overheard the Cobb officer yell, "Hey! Stop right there!"

I could overhear noise on the phone as I ran into the station. I didn't even have to ask, I could tell by the look on the teller's face that it was my old nemesis, the Cobb cut thief.

The Cobb officer came back on the phone and said, "I got the guy!"

I lifted my head from the phone and told the clerk, "We got the guy."

The radiant smile on the clerk's face was ample reward for my services.

I took the clerk over to where the Cobb officer was holding the suspect, and he confirmed that we had the right guy. I moved the suspect from the Cobb County patrol car to mine, got some information from the officer, and drove away.

This was one of the few cases that I ever had go to trial; most perps plea a deal. To give Fulton County District Attorney's Office credit, they prosecuted him as a felony repeat offender. The suspect had several prior convictions and ended up getting a multi-year jail sentence.

I always imagined that cross-jurisdiction cases would be difficult to prosecute, but all I had to do was put the circumstances and Cobb officers' actions in the report, and the legal system did the rest.

In addition to the good case, I made an ally in the Cobb County Police Department

Close Call

I had just come on duty for Day Watch and, before getting into my car, was dispatched to a fight call. The location was in a neighborhood close to the precinct. I hurriedly threw my gear onto the passenger seat and sped to the scene.

Arriving at the address, I saw two women on the sidewalk pointing towards a house. I pulled up and when I got out of the car, one of the women said, "Officer, I was taking a walk and saw a man and woman fighting right here!" pointing down to where we were standing. "The man hit the woman right in the face and then dragged her into the house," she said, pointing a trembling finger towards the house right in front of us.

I called for backup and went towards the front door. As I approached, I heard yelling coming from inside. I listened at the door and heard a man telling a woman to "Shut-up!", and then the voices got lower. Suddenly, the female voiced yelled out and I could tell she was in trouble. I knocked on the door and heard the female say, "Come in."

The door was locked, but the voices, after getting softer, got loud again. I reared back and kicked the door at about the handle level. The door must have been faulty, because it opened on the first kick. I had my gun drawn as I came through the door, and saw a man, about 35-years old, running across the living room towards the back of the house. I could see a young female with a very anguished look on her face laying on a couch.

I called for the man to stop and caught up with him at the back door, literally tackling him as he slowed down to open it. The man tried to force me off him and we wrestled around the kitchen, knocking over chairs and displacing the stove and making a mess of the place. While this was going on, I could hear a constant barrage of calls from Dispatch and my supervisor's, asking, "Two-oh-six, are you okay?" I wanted to yell and tell them to "shut-the-hell-up," but I was a little busy at the time.

I forced the man up against the stove and pulled out my baton. Fortunately, I didn't have to use it--he raised his hands in surrender—he was completely out of gas, and so was I. I pushed him down on the floor and ordered him onto his stomach so I could put handcuffs on him. For about ten seconds I just lay on top of him in order to catch my breath.

I pulled out my radio and tried to transmit that I was okay, but it was hard to get a word in between everyone trying to see if I was okay. Finally, I was able to get a call in, and said, "Everything's fine, I've got one detained." Obviously, that wasn't enough for someone, because after a brief second, I heard, "Two-oh-six, are you okay?" again. Fortunately, back-up officers were coming through the door, and when they saw I was standing, and the perp was cuffed, they did me the favor of calling back, "…yes, Two-oh-six is fine. One detained." If I had made that call, I think I might have said something unkind on the radio (we'll leave it at that).

I took the suspect outside and searched him. He had an I-phone in one of his front pockets, and in a back pocket I found a cell phone battery. I initially thought, "Oh, that's cool, he carries an extra battery so that his phone never runs out of power." I had been having trouble keeping my old droid charged through an entire workday so this seemed a clever solution.

"Oh, you got an extra battery. That's a cool idea," I said.

He smiled and nodded, as if to acknowledge my compliment. However; I quickly realized that the extra battery was for a droid, not an I-phone, and said, "Yep, great idea, but this battery doesn't go to your phone."

"Oh, that battery belongs to a friend; it goes to his phone." he said.

Whenever someone tells me that something they have belongs to a friend or relative, my next question is always, "So, what's your friend's name?"

There was a long hesitation and the suspect's demeaner changed from glad-to-talk to defensive, as he said, "I ain't sayin' no more without my lawyer."

I got the hint, finished my search, and placed him into the back of another officer's patrol car. I then returned to the victim to try and piece the facts of the case together.

By this time, several officers had arrived on scene and the victim told us her story.

"I came over to the house at around three o'clock this morning, to see him," she said. "I'm a model, and he's a photographer, so we were going to do a photo shoot. We had done a shoot last week, and I wanted a few more photos done."

I listened intently as she talked, writing down everything I could.

She hesitated, as if she thought I might say something, then continued. "When I came over this morning, we were talking and he started to touch me," she said, as she arranged herself on the couch into a full sitting position. "He said he wanted to have sex with me again, but I wasn't in the mood."

Again, she looked at me as if to see if I was going to ask her anything, but I just nodded, and said, "Please, continue."

"Well, he eventually pulled his penis out of his pants and I told him no, so he put it back in. I told him that I wasn't in the mood, so I got up and left the house to make a phone call and get a ride home."

She seemed to be thinking of what to say next so I tried to help her, asking, "What happened after you left the house?"

"As I was standing out on the sidewalk, making a phone call, he came running out of the house screaming at me and grabbed my arm, trying to get me back into the house. I tried to pull away, but he's strong, and he hit me on the face! I remember my earrings came off and he dragged me back into the house.

When we got back into the house, I knew he was going to rape me. He took my phone and pulled the battery out and stuck the battery in his back pocket. Then he held is hand over my mouth. If y'all hadn't arrived, I'm sure he would have raped me," she said, tears streaming down her face.

Sure enough, we found two large hoop earrings on the sidewalk where the fight had occurred, hair extensions on the porch, and, of course, I found the cell phone battery in his back pocket.

Her story made sense (except for her coming to his house at 0300 hours for "photos" and the whole he-wanted-to-have-sex-with-me-again-but-I-wasn't-in-the-mood thing). I was tempted to delve a little deeper into the story, but the zone investigators and Sex Crime unit had arrived; they could take it from here.

Stories like hers are fairly common in law enforcement and you want to sympathize with the victim, but at the same time you want to tell them, "What were you thinking?" However, her story was just the tip of the iceberg; the future held stories, scenarios, and a web of lies that would make her narrative sound totally reasonable.

Arresting Lieutenant Williams

One complaint I often get during traffic stops goes something like this: 'Why don't you go catch some real criminals instead of pulling over innocent people.' Also, if I'm at a party or a gathering where people learn that I'm a police officer, there's always someone who will tell me about the time they were pulled over even though they hadn't broken any laws. I used to try to explain to them that cops are not pulling people over just for the fun of it. Or, the cop probably didn't know you were black, or female, or gay, when they pulled you over; however, I found that this usually ended up with me listening to more stories of supposed police abuse. I'm not saying there aren't bad cops. Of course, there are bad cops, just like there are bad teachers, lawyers, preachers, priests, you-name-it. But the vast majority of police officers and deputies, I'd estimate above 95%, are good people trying to do a good job.

Now when people tell me about how they were pulled over for no reason, I say something along the lines of, "We get a lot of bad people off the streets during traffic stops because bad people not only rob, kill, and steal, they also don't care about other laws—especially, traffic laws." Here's an example:

During a morning rollcall briefing, we were given a BOLO (be on the lookout) poster on a homicide suspect. He was also wanted for aggravated assault, forgery and kidnapping. We were told that an FBI task force was in town because they had good intelligence that the suspect was in Atlanta.

As I looked at the poster, there was something very familiar about the suspect; I had seen this guy before. All of a sudden, I realized something, and said aloud, "This guy looks just like Lieutenant Williams!"

Everyone in the room agreed that the perp had a strong resemblance to a Lieutenant Williams who had retired a year earlier. We laughed about the resemblance and then went out to our beats.

About thirty minutes later, while it was still dark, I saw a car driving down Chattahoochee Avenue with its headlights off. I pulled the car over, and as soon as I saw the driver I thought, "Damn! It's Lieutenant Williams."

But it wasn't Lieutenant Williams.

Without identifying myself, or even extending a greeting, I said, "Sir, could you turn off the car and hand me the keys?"

He complied.

Then, opening the car door, I said, "Sir, could you undo your seatbelt?"

He complied.

"Sir, lean forward, please, and put your left hand behind your back."

"You mean like this?" the man said as he did what I requested.

I quickly got both arms in cuffs, and the man's expression changed from mild bewilderment to resignation. He then let out a slow and prolonged, "Daaamn!"

Once I had him in my patrol car, I confirmed he was the suspect the FBI was looking for. The FBI task force arrived within five minutes of me announcing his arrest over the radio.

The task force pulled three handguns out of the suspect's car. Later I was told that when the task force went to the suspect's hotel room, there was a woman bound, gagged and tied to the bed. In addition, they recovered large amounts of drugs, hundreds of fake credit cards, and a machine that makes credit cards.

As we were driving to jail the suspect asked, "How in the hell did you know it was me?"

"Well, I really arrested you by mistake: I thought you were Lieutenant Williams, an old boss of mine, and I was playing a trick on you," I said, in an attempt at humor.

"You really surprised me," the suspect said. After a short hesitation he said, "Good thing you surprised me; if you hadn't, we would have had a problem."

If I had a dollar for every perp I've caught because of a traffic stop…I'd have a lot of dollars.

Five Feet, Twelve Inches

I pulled over a young woman for speeding and she said she didn't have her license on her. She also said she didn't have a photo ID with her. Atlanta Police policy states that if we can't readily identify someone who's committed an illegal act, we should take them to the jail to be positively identified and post bond; basically, arrest them. However, depending on the circumstances, I usually get their identifying data and then run them on my patrol car computer. If they have a Facebook page or some other social media, I can often verify their information through that. If their information comes back as valid, I'll issue the necessary citations, including a citation for not having their license on them. I asked her the typical identifying questions, and nothing seemed amiss until I asked her how tall she was.

"Five-eleven, five-twelve," she answered.

Thinking I hadn't heard her correctly, I asked her to repeat herself.

"About five-twelve," she confidently said.

I'm six feet tall and have been since my sophomore year of high school, but I have never referred to myself as five-feet-twelve-inches tall, so I knew she was lying about her identity. I took down her information as if it was the gospel truth, then went back to my car. I ran the name and date of birth in the computer, and it came back to a woman with a valid license and matching address. However; the height on my computer was 5'-09".

I went back to the woman's car and asked for her keys. I then asked that she get out of the car. As she got out, I saw that the woman who had said she was 5'-12" was closer to 5'-05" tall.

"Ma'am, turn around, please, and put your hands behind your back," I said.

The woman became quite upset, and said, "I'm sorry, I got confused. I gave you my sister's name and information by mistake. Please, please, don't take me to jail!"

"Ma'am," I began, as I was about to tell her that using someone else's identity information was a serious offense because it could lead to an arrest warrant against the wrong person, I was cut short.

Just when I had the cuffs on her, she turned around and said in a sexy low tone, "Officer, I'll do anything to stay out of jail. You're kind of cute, and I think I know what you'd like." With the last word, she moved closer (we were already only inches apart) and looked up at me with a Come-Hither gaze. However, when she realized that her tactic had failed, she began to cry, saying, "...this is going to ruin my life!"

I assured her that this wouldn't ruin her life, concluding with, "But it could have really affected your sister's life if you had gotten away with it."

I called for a female officer to come and search the woman. When I told the officer, who was from Haiti, about how I had known the woman was lying, she said, "I've got a whole lot of Blonde jokes going through my head right now, and her face is stamped on every one of them."

We both laughed at her comment, and I was still smiling when I walked back and got in the patrol car.

"What in the hell are you so happy about? You're glad when you can ruin someone's life..." the woman said as she settled into full-fledged rage.

I couldn't help it, (I was still smiling) and I explained to her that I thought it was humorous that she described herself as 5'-12", and how it made me suspicious that she was not who she said she was. She obviously didn't understand what was wrong with saying 5'-12", as opposed to 6-feet, and then, realizing I was not going to change my mind about arresting her, vehemently denied that she had said she was 5'-12", claiming she had said 5'-05" and threatening to sue me.

Her alibi made me smile even more, and I actually laughed, probably a little too loud, as she went into a tirade about me being a "sadistic misogynous," happy to lock up innocent girls. Later I looked up the word "misogynous." Once again, she was wrong.

Realizing she didn't understand why her use of the term "5'-12"" made me suspicious, I came up with an analogy, explaining, "Saying you're 5'-12" would be like saying, "I'm 312 months old" instead of "I'm 26 years old."

She was still fuming, claiming I was a liar, when we got to the jail. I was going to let her believe what she wanted but then had a change of heart. I keyed up the patrol car video and turned it so she could see and hear it in the back of the car. I replayed her saying she was 5'-12" not only once, but twice.

She was a much more subdued 5"-12" when I walked her into the jail.

I don't like putting people in jail, not because they don't deserve it but because it makes for a lot of work and it probably doesn't change most people's behavior. I think the vast majority of traffic violations are just honest mistakes, and most officers feel the same. I have been pulled over for speeding at least a half dozen times (I like to drive fast), and in each one of those incidents I could have been jailed—I can only imagine how bad I'd feel if I had been arrested in any of those instances. However, a traffic infraction goes from "honest mistake" to outright wrong-doing when someone lies about their identity or tries to obstruct the officer. In fact, I let about half of the people I pull over get off with a verbal warning, as many of the cops I know do, so there's little reason for the average citizen to lie or physically resist when they get pulled over.

In the State of Georgia, all traffic violations are criminal offenses and the officer has the discretion to either take or not take the violator to jail to post bond. So, when someone commits an honest mistake, like speeding at ten to twenty miles over the limit or running a stop light, they need to keep in mind that jail is an option—and jail's almost a certainty if the officer catches them trying to disguise their identity.

Take this woman as an example; if she had gotten away with convincing me that she was her sister, and if she hadn't paid the fine or gone to court, her sister's license would have been suspended. In that case, the next time the sister got pulled over for even a minor offense, the sister would have, at the very least, been given a citation for driving with a suspended license. At worst, she would be taken to jail through no fault of her own.

In this case, I was happy to be taking this woman to jail to post bond. I'd like to believe that this was a wakeup call for her.

Her Crip Boyfriend

I was dispatched on a stolen car call, and the victim told me that her boyfriend had taken her car about 5 days ago, and it had been stolen while he was in a bad part of town. Her frustration with her boyfriend was visible as she told me how he had waited four days to tell her about the stolen car, because he was trying to solve the case himself and get the car back. She showed me the rental agreement, and I explained to her that I couldn't do a stolen auto report at that time because I would need the testimony of her boyfriend.

The woman's frustration level rose as she asked me why, as the sole lessee, she couldn't report it stolen right now. I said she could if she could get her boyfriend on the scene to tell me exactly where, when, and under what circumstances the car was taken. The woman said her boyfriend was at work and wouldn't be available until 5 o'clock. I tried to explain that I would need both of them in order to do a report, but she wasn't taking "no" for an answer.

Her frustration rose to anger as she accused me of not wanting to do my job. I tried to get a supervisor to come out, but all three of them were working emergency situations and wouldn't be available for some time. I tried to convince her to contact City Dispatch or my precinct for further clarification, but she refused to call anyone; she wanted someone to come and take care of her situation now. I put the supervisor request in anyway, and then asked a female officer to come to the scene. Maybe a female could explain the situation in a way the woman would accept.

Officer Amore, a very calm and knowledgeable officer, came, but after about 15 minutes Amore still couldn't get through to the woman.

Up to this point I was starting to think, "Is it me? Is there something or someway I'm behaving that is making it hard for this woman to understand?" No, Officer Amore had told her pretty much the same things I told her, and the lady didn't understand. Worse still, when we told the lady we couldn't take the report because, as far as we knew, her boyfriend could be legitimately driving around town in the car, just telling her it was stolen as a cover story, she became incensed.

"My boyfriend used to be with the Crips, but he's given up all that! Do you think a black man who's given up The Life would drive around in a potentially stolen car? You must be crazy..." she said.

Finally, after about 2 hours, a sergeant was able to arrive on scene. I watched from a distance as the sergeant listened to the lady tell her story. I could see the woman's anger rise and could tell the sergeant was saying the same things Officer Amore and I had said. After about 20 minutes I saw the sergeant start to walk away from the lady as he keyed up his radio. This is what the sergeant said on the radio: "Unit 2293 to Radio. For the record, the victim gave her car to her Crip boyfriend and he has a legitimate right to drive the vehicle. Code 12 (no report)."

Mr. Reynolds

I got dispatched to a restaurant where a customer had walked out without paying his $82 bill. As I pulled up to the front, the manager was standing outside on the sidewalk pointing his finger down the street, saying, "That dude in the brown shirt and dark pants just walked out without paying!"

As I started up the street to confront the suspect, he turned around and headed back towards us. The suspect gave me a big smile as he approached and held out his hand to shake as if we were old friends.

"I sure am glad to see you," he began. "I told these people I was just going up to the ATM because my credit card isn't working. I was coming right back!"

The man, Mr. Reynolds, went on to plead his case, and stressed that he was just in town for business. Mr. Reynolds was tall, well dressed and well spoken, with a deep, resonant, baritone voice.

I talked to the manager who told me that Mr. Reynolds had been in the restaurant for over three hours, ordering the most expensive dinner on the menu, ordering drinks and desserts, and even buying a drink for someone at another table. The manager said that Mr. Reynolds was on the phone most of the time, speaking loudly and seemingly making business deals; he was even on the phone while they were dealing with him about the bill.

"We tried several times to settle his bill earlier and he kept saying that he was waiting on someone," the manager said.

Occasionally, Mr. Reynolds would interject, 'Well, I can assure you that I was waiting on someone...I resent that I'm being treated like a common criminal....'

The manager went on to tell me how Mr. Reynolds had driven the restaurant staff crazy trying to wait on him, and then blamed them when his credit card was rejected. Mr. Reynolds would interject an occasional protest as the manager told me they were insisting that he pay up now.

"Well, I guess I could get my uncle, Major West, to come and bring me some money," Mr. Reynolds said. "He's a Major in the Atlanta Police Department."

"Would that work for you?" I asked the manager.

"Sure, if he gets here before we close in an hour."

I had Mr. Reynolds call his uncle, and while he did that, I called one of the sergeants back at the precinct to see if they knew a Major West. The sergeant assured me that he had never heard of "Major West", and concluded by saying, "If there is one, he must have retired many years ago."

Not surprisingly, Mr. Reynolds said he could not reach his uncle.

"Well, is there anyone else in town that you could call?" I asked.

"No. I can't think of anyone else. But I know my uncle would be down here in just a few minutes if I could get in touch with him."

I let Mr. Reynolds continue trying to reach his uncle while I talked to the manager. The manager was visibly upset about the situation, and I could tell he was intimidated by the much larger and smooth-talking Mr. Reynolds. But he was adamant that Mr. Reynolds either pay or go to jail. I finally convinced Mr. Reynolds to get off the phone and placed him in handcuffs.

On the way to jail, Mr. Reynolds kept making big claims about how much money he made and that his credit card didn't work because he just got back from Switzerland, and they must have put a lock on his card, because he hadn't informed them he was coming back to the United States this early.

I was feeling sorry for Mr. Reynolds because his claims seemed believable on the surface, but then I realized that if he was such a seasoned traveler, wouldn't he have had more than one credit card? Also, why didn't he have the foresight to get money from the ATM earlier? Just then we were passing a bank with several ATMs and I asked Mr. Reynolds if he wanted to stop and get some cash; maybe we could go back and pay for the dinner and this entire "misunderstanding" would be over.

"Nah, that's alright," he said.

I didn't say anything in response. At that point I was sure he was just a con man, a very convincing one, just trying to live the high life.

The average person would not believe how often people lie to the police. I came to the point that I did not believe anyone I encountered on the streets. I only believed what could be proved by documentation or an objective third party. It may seem cynical, but it's usually the best way to do business as a police officer.

Chapter 6. Liar-Liar

My Cousin's Car

I was driving down a one-way street and observed a Mazda sedan parked in the middle of the road, facing the wrong way. I activated my patrol car lights, pulled in front of the car, and approached. The driver acted apologetic and said he was waiting on a friend who was a mechanic--he was supposed to meet the friend at this location. I asked him for his driver's license and he told me that he didn't have his license on him. He appeared very nervous.

I ran the car plate and discovered the vehicle he was driving was stolen out of a nearby County. When I asked him if he owned the car, he said, no, that it was his cousin's. When I asked for his cousin's name, he said he didn't know it, but everyone called him Ray-ray."

I then asked where he was coming from, and he stated that he was coming from Douglasville and his cousin gave him the car because the car had a vibration problem. He explained that he was waiting for his mechanic friend to come and diagnose the problem.

I asked the man to call his friend. He tried to call the mechanic multiple times and each time the man told me his friend was on the way. On at least two occasions he said, "He says he'll be here in ten minutes."

Suddenly, the man's story changed. Instead of belonging to his cousin, he said the car was a rental. He explained that his cousin had rented it and then had a small accident, and they wanted to get the car fixed before taking it back to the rental company.

"What rental company is the car from?" I asked.

Without hesitation the man said the car came from Chris Auto Sells.

I knew Chris Auto Sells to be a real company in Atlanta so I pulled out my phone to give them a call. As I started to place the call, the man changed his story again and said, "No, I got confused, the company is Hertz."

"Do you have the paperwork for the rental?" I asked.

The man was about to say something but stopped in mid-breath, looked down towards the ground, blew out a lung full of air, and said, "You got me." Then, he stuck his arms out in front of him, indicating that I should put handcuffs on him.

Later, as I was processing him for jail, he said, "You know, the older I get, the harder it gets to keep a story together."

"I know what you mean; it gets harder to string a series of lies together."

I heard the man quietly say, "Yep."

Ain't My Pants

My first call of the day was to a dispute at a sleazy motel. When I arrived, the security guard said that a guy they had warned several times to stay off the premises was back and arguing with another guest. The guard said that when she intervened, the subject cursed her out and wouldn't leave.

I found the suspect in front of the motel by a bus stop. He pleaded his innocence, but I had a written statement from the guard and arrested him. He had the strongest smell of alcohol on his breath that I have ever smelled. We were outside, and the smell was very noticeable even from several feet away. When I searched him, I found steel wool (often used as a filter in drug pipes) in his pocket.

"What's this for?" I asked.

"I don't know what that is? These aren't even my pants!"

"Whose pants are they?"

"I don't know, but they ain't mine," he answered.

When I checked the other front pocket, I found a small plastic bag of crack cocaine and a glass tube, used as a pipe. Without me asking, the man said, "I told you man, these ain't even my pants!"

"Well then, whose pants are they?" I asked.

I was certain he'd say, "They're my cousin's pants," but he just dropped his head and shook it side-to-side.

I've gotten to the point that if someone tells me that something is their cousin's (whether it be pants, a car, a gun, a Bible, whatever), I know for sure that they're lying, and the item is, indeed, theirs.

He asked me what I was charging him with, and I told him "Criminal Trespassing, Possession, and Disorderly Conduct."

"Criminal Trespassing? I ain't no criminal!" he said, slurring his words.

He was somewhat of a jailhouse lawyer and proceeded to explain that I had no grounds to charge him as "a criminal." I tried to explain to him that the term is just what the State calls it, but he wanted no part of being "a criminal."

After he complained some more, I said, "Okay, I'll just cite you for regular trespassing."

He immediately calmed down. It was still the same charge, in fact, it was the least of his charges, but by not calling it "criminal" it seemed to make him feel better.

Later, when I checked the suspect's criminal history, I saw that he had been convicted of burglary and drug possession and had done time in prison. I guess those pants actually were his.

Sock Puppets

One afternoon in May, another officer and I were dispatched to a Burglar in a Residence call. Dispatch advised that an anonymous caller reported that three black males, one of which was light-skinned, had entered the residence from the rear door and that the owners were out of town.

We arrived on scene, and the other officer told me to cover the front of the residence while he went to the back. I'd been standing to the side of the front porch for a few seconds and suddenly saw a couple of faces appear, then disappear, at a large plate-glass window. We had gotten radio silence so the frequency was open for me to let the other officer know there were definitely people in the house.

"I know," the other officer said, "I've got two of them at gun point."

I waited a moment for him to say something else, then, not hearing anything, ran to join up with him.

"Did you get the other guy?" he said excitedly as he held his gun on two young men with their hands in the air and socks over each hand, like sock puppets.

"What other guy?" I answered.

The other officer smiled, and as we were cuffing the perps, he explained how he had found the back door ajar and could see three guys, with socks on their hands, going through the drawers of a dining room set. "One of the guys ran, and these two guys stuck their hands up."

After securing our two suspects, we cleared the house and found where the third suspect had escaped through a side window.

In questioning the suspects, they said that they had just followed the third guy into the house, thinking that the guy lived there. "We had no idea that he was going to steal anything!" they said.

"Yeah, man, we just met him on the street and he said he had some weed. We was (sic) just gonna smoke some weed. I swear on my mama!"

We didn't have the heart to point out to the suspects that with socks over their hands, so as not to leave prints, their story was not very convincing.

The victims eventually arrived and the suspects were found to have several stolen items in their pockets.

My Cousin's Jacket

I was dispatched to a shoplifting call at a convenience store. Dispatch advised that there was a group of children who had stolen items from the store. En route, I noticed several kids, who matched the descriptions given by Dispatch, walking down the street. I pulled over and asked the first boy where they were coming from.

"We just came from over there," he said, pointing in the direction of the store. I approached the kid and advised him that I was going to detain him. As I reached for him, he started to turn away. I was lucky enough to catch his wrist and hand as he started to run, and quickly got him under control and cuffed. The other kids ran, and I put out a quick BOLO over the radio.

I found a couple of wrapped candy bars in his hoodie pocket. "Where did you get these?" I asked.

"I don't know, man. I didn't know those were there," he explained.

"How do you not know you have candy bars in your hoodie pocket?"

"I swear, man, on my mom's (sic), that I didn't know. This ain't even my jacket!" he answered. "It's my cousin's jacket."

I continued my search and he became very upset, shouting vulgarities and twisting his body away. I eventually recovered several more candy bars, a can of soda, and cigarettes from his pant pockets.

After I had the kid in my backseat and was completing some paperwork, an older man, in his twenties, approached, saying that he was the kid's brother. By this time, I had already gotten the kid's name, but I asked the older man, "What is your brother's name?"

The man thought for a second and then said a name. I also asked for a birthdate, but the name and the birthdate didn't match on my computer. The older man appeared to be wanting to help, or at least get an explanation, so I got out of my car in order to talk to him away from the kid.

"Alright, sir. That name and birthdate don't come up on my computer. Are you sure you got the birthdate correct?" I asked.

"Well, I might have the date wrong," he started, and then, switching into high gear, started yelling, "This is bulls--

t, man. F--k this s--t! You just pulled up on him and arrested him cause he's black. You (sic) a bitch, man!"

The man continued swearing and I finally said, "Sir, I need you to leave the area. You're not helping the situation, and all you're going to get, here, is trouble."

About this time another patrol car pulled up and the man, glancing at the car, started walking away, cursing and throwing his hands up in the air as he left.

I drove over to the store and about fifteen minutes later, while speaking with the cashier, the same man, who'd advised me he was the suspect's brother, approached. He started to talk, but I asked him to wait a minute while I talked to the cashier. Obviously, he couldn't wait a minute and proceeded to curse at me and the cashier. At that point I turned to him and, again, told him to leave.

"F--k you, man," he continued, "You just a bitch-ass n----r..."

Again, I warned the man to leave the store or be arrested for obstruction, but he continued, putting his arms out to his sides, as if he wanted to fight, and then hitching up his pants. When he went to hitch up his pants for about the third time, I grabbed his right wrist and quickly got it behind his back. He continued to struggle, but I had a good hold and was able to wrestle him to the ground and get cuffs on him without too much additional drama.

After going through a litany of false names and birthdates, I finally got good information on both suspects.

They weren't brothers. However, I've heard they were boyfriends in jail (just a rumor).

The moral of this story is, when an officer asks you to leave a scene, he's trying to do you a favor. Most cops don't want to make small-time arrests--the paperwork makes us late getting home--but if you insist on going to jail, we are happy to oblige.

World's Best Salesman

Early one morning, around three o'clock, I was sitting in my patrol car in a parking lot on Piedmont Road when I saw an SUV cross the six-lane road by driving over a raised median. It was the usual time bars closed in Atlanta, so I expected I had a possible DUI situation. I, too, had to cross the raised median as I attempted to catch up to the driver (not illegal for police when carrying out their duties). The car was doing the speed limit as I followed, and I saw no signs of weaving. However, I had plenty of probable cause to pull the car over because it had a "Test Drive" license plate, and I had seen the vehicle illegally cross over the median.

I pulled the car over and was greeted by a friendly sixty-one-year-old black man, Oscar Smith (I cannot remember his real name). Oscar looked like a typical man in his sixties, gray thinning hair and a little heavier than average, but he had a twinkle in his eyes and a smile that was very appealing.

As I started to explain why I had pulled him over, Mr. Smith said, "Oh, Officer, you wouldn't believe the week I've had."

"Okay, give me a try?" I said, concerned for the man as he lowered his head and shook it side-to-side towards the end of his sentence. I saw a glimmer of tears well up in his eyes, and for a moment thought he might break down. His demeanor switched from jovial to concerned and sad almost immediately, but he maintained a semblance of composure.

"I went to Hennessy Lexus and they let me take this car for a three-day test drive on Friday, but early Sunday morning I started to have a very sharp pain in my side," he said as he motioned towards his right side. "I was really worried that I might be getting sick, you know. I'm a Deacon and I teach Sunday School at Elizabeth Oaks Baptist Church, and I know they'd be in a hurt if I didn't show up," he said.

At the time, I was playing in the praise-band of my church and I could sympathize with his predicament. "Yeah, I can see how that could be a problem," I commented.

"Those boys need someone to look up to—they're really not boys, they're young men--and if I'm not there to teach them about The Lord, well it would break their hearts. They need me," he said, never looking away from me as he spoke. "Anyway, I called my buddy, Bobo, and he took me to the emergency room at Northside Hospital. Praise the Lord for Bobo, because I couldn't have driven myself, you know.   Anyway, the doctor told me I had a ruptured appendix."

Mr. Smith would look intently at me every time he said "you know," squinting his eyes, raising his right hand up to his waist with the index finger partially extended, in a way that indicated "you know" wasn't just a verbal quirk, rather, he was honestly hoping I'd understand.

"They immediately put me in the hospital. Bobo said he'd take the car back home and park it in my driveway. He even said he'd take it back to Hennessy on Monday. Well, Bobo is a good old boy, like a brother, but he has a son, twenty years old, who has had some trouble, you know. I don't know how Bobo does it, but he loves that boy. Anyway, while I was in the hospital and, unbeknownst to me, Bobo's son took the car to Tennessee and was there for three days! I had surgery Sunday afternoon so I was kind of out of it. I was hoping to get out on Monday but I got an infection. They tried to fight it with antibiotics, but they had to go back in to operate on Tuesday. Long story short, I didn't get home until last night at eight."

At this point, Mr. Smith looked up at me with a sad expression, saying, "It's a mess; when I got home, I found the car still in my driveway. Bobo told me what had happened, and I tried to call Hennessy last night. I left a message, but they were closed. I plan on taking the car back first thing this morning, but around midnight I was starting to feel a lot of pain, not in my side but down my left leg. I just couldn't stand it anymore so I'm just now coming from the all-night pharmacy at Kroger."

Mr. Smith lifted his shirt to show me a long bandage extending from the middle of his stomach to his right side. "You see, I still have the dressing on. Here's my bag of medicines and bandages," he said as he showed me a black leather pouch that had been sitting in the passenger seat.

I took a quick peek into the pouch, but only to check it for weapons. I hadn't run the license plate because it was a "Test Drive" tag.

"Well, I'm really sorry for all this, let me just run your VIN and see what we got," I said, trying to sound optimistic as Mr. Smith handed me his license.

Usually, when someone's lying during a traffic stop, they are much more demonstrative than Mr. Smith had been, raising their voice, swearing and gesturing, and they will often trip up and say something that doesn't make sense. Mr. Smith hadn't done any of that, and his story made sense. In addition, I had been a cop for less than a year, and I believed him.

The one thing going against Mr. Smith, and in the City's favor, was that I'm an obsessive person and like to research. When I got back to my patrol car, I found that Mr. Smith's license was legitimate and he didn't have any warrants. However, when I ran the VIN, the car came back as stolen. I checked the date it was reported and, sure enough, it matched Monday's date. Furthermore, Hennessy

Lexus was the Reporting Party. I also researched Hennessy Lexus to see if it was a local dealer. (At that time, the only "Hennessy" I knew of was a liquor.) I found they were located on Peachtree Industrial Boulevard. I also googled "Elizabeth Oaks Baptist Church" and an Elizabeth Baptist Church in Atlanta came back. Close enough.

I sat in my car, disappointed that the SUV had come back as stolen. Mr. Smith seemed like a good guy who had fallen on some bad luck. I didn't bother looking for Mr. Smith's criminal background, it didn't really matter because Mr. Smith had been found driving a stolen auto, a felony, and I had to arrest him.

I called for the paddy wagon and a tow truck to impound the SUV.

"Okay, Mr. Smith. This car definitely comes back on my computer as stolen," I said when I returned to his car.

"Yeah, I was afraid of that," he replied.

I didn't take Mr. Smith out of the vehicle, because I just didn't have the heart for it. Instead, I took his keys and said, "Just sit tight here in the car. The paddy wagon is on the way and they'll take you to jail."

"I'm really sorry for all this trouble," Mr. Smith commented. "I just feel horrible about this situation."

He appeared to be really despondent, and his occasional gasps, as if he was in pain, didn't make me feel any better about the situation.

The paddy wagon must have been in the area because it showed up after a couple of minutes. I told the transporting officer about what had happened and handed him the citations he'd need to put Mr. Smith in jail. "I'll send you a copy of the report on email as soon as I get it," I assured the officer.

(When I first became a police officer we could arrest and take people to jail, caught in the act of a crime, without a written warrant. Later, the arrest process for felonies became much more difficult because we were required to get a warrant from a magistrate judge. This process involved taking the arrestee back to the precinct and using a computer program to fill out a long application and then talk to the magistrate via the computer. The process also required us to talk to the Fulton County District Attorney's Office. In short, it was difficult, unless you made a lot of felony arrests and did it often. It added at least an hour to every felony arrest, sometimes up to three hours if the judge was busy. Suffice it to say, the number of arrests probably decreased considerably when this new process was implemented.)

As Mr. Smith was getting into the wagon, I said, "Good luck. I'm sure Hennessy won't prosecute once they hear what happened."

Mr. Smith smiled and said, "Oh, I'm sure they will understand." He then laughed softly. "It's just part of life. You take the good with the bad, and praise God for his many blessings."

I went back to my patrol car to wait for the tow truck.

When I got back to the precinct at the end of my shift, the paddy wagon officer came up to me, saying, "You know that old dude who was found in the stolen SUV, the one that had a story about being in the hospital?"

"Yeah. What's the word?"

"I had to take him to Grady Detention because the jail wouldn't take him with his medical condition. When they were checking him out at Grady, they removed the bandage on his stomach and found that there was no scar, no injury, no nothing underneath. It was a prop! And that black bag he said had medicine in it was only filled with trash. I ran his name through the database and he has over thirty arrests for receiving stolen property and theft.

"You're kidding," I said, amazed at this revelation.

"Yeah, he was telling me his story on the way to the jail, and I was half believing him!" the officer said with a wide smile. The wagon driver seemed just as amazed as I was.

Later, I saw Mr. Smith's criminal history. There it was in black and white; Mr. Smith had a spreadsheet of over sixty pages and he'd spent half of his life in prison. He was a life-long criminal and the best liar I'd ever encountered.

I couldn't help but think how successful Mr. Smith could have been as an honest salesman.

Chapter 7. Dirty Jobs

Striptease in the Woods

I was on patrol on a rainy day when I spotted a sedan with an expired license plate. I tried to pull the car over but the driver hit the gas. With my lights and siren on, I started to chase the suspect but quickly realized, with the rain and heavy Atlanta traffic, I would be putting others at risk. I turned off my lights and siren and proceeded to follow in the general direction of the car even after losing sight of it. I announced my situation on the radio and heard a couple of other units say they were headed my way.

A few minutes later I came upon the car stopped in a center lane of Lenox Road, with the driver's door hanging open, and caught a glimpse of a man running into the woods. I stopped behind the car and made chase, advising other units of what was going on. The man had at least a hundred-yard head start on me, but I continued to run as fast as my fifty-five-year-old body would let me.

After a few minutes I came across the driver's shirt, tossed on a tree branch, and grabbed it as I ran by. A minute later I came across a pair of shorts and one shoe and grabbed those also. Over the next 4-6 minutes, I recovered another shoe, ball cap, socks, and shorts, grabbing them and letting radio know that the suspect was now probably running in his underwear. I was tempted to add some humor to the call and tell Dispatch, "He's naked, and running," but I was too wet and winded to see any humor in the situation. It had been raining most of the day and the wet leaves and branches were soaking me.

The chase led up a hill to the back of a house, and I noticed police car lights on the street in front of the house. "Great, those guys have probably already got him," I thought.

As I came around a corner of the house, I was surprised to see the suspect just a few feet in front of me, running back towards me, wearing only his white briefs. Instinctively I threw up my arm and clotheslined the suspect, dropping him into a shallow muddy depression. When I clotheslined him, the shoes in my hand gave him a good whack on the face and he was momentarily stunned.

He rolled around in the mud for a few seconds as I ordered him to stay down. I didn't want to wrestle with him in the mud, so the next time he tried to get up I pepper sprayed him. The spray had an immediate effect and the suspect yelled and dropped back down. Nonetheless, he tried to get up again. Just then, another officer came from the front of the house and yelled for the suspect to stay down. The suspect tried to get up again and the officer, in an effort to avoid a mud bath, pulled out his baton and pushed it against the suspect's back to keep him down. By now, the suspect was acting like a mad-man, flailing around in the mud in an attempt to get away. This went on for a few seconds, with the officer pushing him back down each time he tried to get up. Eventually, a sergeant came by and the three of us were able to subdue the suspect, but not before we were covered in mud from head to foot.

When it was all over, we looked at ourselves and realized we would have to get cleaned up before doing anymore policing; we looked like swamp creatures. As bad as we looked, the suspect looked even worse, like he'd been living in the mud for days. The only places he wasn't covered in mud were his eyeballs and teeth.

We ended up cleaning ourselves and the suspect off with a garden hose. It took me two days to get my utility belt clean and dry.

Pass the Pepper

I was dispatched to a trespassing call at a moving company. When I arrived, I saw a young man and an older woman at the front door of the company, arguing with a man who was standing in the doorway. The woman appeared to be trying to pull the teen away from the man.

As I approached, the teen pulled away from the woman and walked towards me.

"He won't pay me my money!" he said, as I pulled out my note pad.

The teen was very upset and told me he had shown up for work and the boss, the man he'd been arguing with, had told him to leave. "But I ain't leaving until he pays me for this week!" the man yelled.

As I was talking to the young man, the woman approached and started to explain that she was there to help her son get "his money," but the owner wouldn't give it to him. As the woman talked the young man became increasingly upset, clenching and unclenching his fists and blowing his cheeks out like a prize fighter waiting for the bell.

I turned towards the teen and tried to ask what his issue was, but he made as if to charge towards his boss, at which point his mom grabbed him.

"I've been trying to get my son to calm down..." she said, as the son tried to pull away from her.

After several minutes, repeatedly placing my body between the teen and his boss, I got the teen settled down a little and convinced him to stay with his mother while I went to talk to his boss.

The owner of the moving company explained that the young man was one of his employees. He said the teen came to work that morning, but was dressed inappropriately, in shorts and a t-shirt. He said the teen was very aware that the moving company required employees to be dressed in a company polo with long pants. "I sent him home because he wasn't dressed appropriately, but he refused to leave. My foreman and I talked to him for over an hour, even convincing him to leave the premises once, but he came right back and demanded his weekly check. I explained to him that checks don't come out until 4 o'clock but he refused to leave without it. We've been trying to get him to leave for over an hour and a half."

I talked separately to the foreman and he gave the same story as the owner.

The owner said he wouldn't press trespassing charges if the teen would leave and agreed to pay him later in the day, at 4 o'clock.

I explained the situation to the teen and his mother, for the umpteenth time, but he was adamant that he wasn't leaving without his check. After conferring with the owner again, I came back to the teen and was surprised to see three more adults with him, two men and a woman. I didn't know what role these newcomers had in this unfolding drama, but, as I was explaining to the teen and his mother that he had to leave or be arrested, the three adults became increasingly vocal.

I tried to deescalate the situation by assuring them that I didn't want to arrest anybody, but their histrionics emboldened the teen to try and charge at the owner again. His mother grabbed him and I tried to put handcuffs on him. During the struggle the mother kept pushing me away and yelling at her son, "Let's just get out of here!"

Up to this point, I would have gladly let the teen and his mom leave without making an arrest; that would have solved all of our problems. However, the teen refused to leave and Mom refused to let me deal with him. Trespassing is generally not a huge deal, but this incident had gone well beyond trespassing.

I told the mother to let go of her son, that he was under arrest, but she was determined to drag him away. Basically, the son was trying to assault the owner, I was trying to make an arrest, and the mother was trying to pull the young man away from me and the owner. Making matters worse, the other adults had decided to get involved and pull me away from the kid. I made several pleas for the adults to back off. I tried to call for backup, but it was all I could do to keep hold of the teen. At that point I was out of options and pulled the pepper spray from my belt. The three adults saw what I was doing and backed off. However, the son and mother got the full can, and they settled to the pavement like Wicked Witches of the West.

"Wow, this stuff really works," I thought.

I got some of spray on myself and called for backup and an ambulance.

I stood over the young man and his mom, keeping my hand on the kid's shoulder as I struggled to cry the pepper spray out of my eyes. Fortunately, I was able to see well enough to get handcuffs on both of them.

After a couple of minutes, a fire engine and another officer arrived.

The firemen tried to wash the spray out of the suspect's eyes. I didn't take any water and was relieved to see that my eyes were fine after about fifteen minutes of letting my tears flush them out.

I still couldn't see very well as I told the other officer what had happened. The other officer asked me if I wanted to arrest the three adults for obstruction. "Sure, but I think they're long gone," I said.

A few other officers had arrived, and I overheard the other officer say, "Arrest them all. All three of them."

Apparently, the three adults had stayed on the scene and were yelling their grievances at the other officers, so everyone knew who they were. The other officer later told me how glad he was when I told him to arrest the three adults.

I continued with my investigation and learned that the other woman was the teen's sister, one of the adult men was his father, and the other was his brother. None of them lived together, but that day they had a family reunion in the back of the paddy wagon.

Racist Radio

Late one night, around two a.m., I was driving through a predominately Hispanic apartment complex and saw 3 guys carrying beer towards a Honda Civic. They spotted me as they were getting in the vehicle, said something in Spanish amongst themselves, then turned and went back into an apartment.

Out of curiosity, I ran the car's tag on my computer and the Civic came back as not insured. I drove about 200 yards down the street and parked so I could complete some paperwork.

After about five minutes, the Civic drove by. Knowing that the vehicle wasn't insured, I activated my blue lights and tried to pull it over. I called Dispatch, telling them I was trying to pull over a vehicle with three Hispanics in it.

The car continued another 300 yards before turning into a parking lot and coming to a stop. As I approached the car, the driver started to get out. I yelled for him to stay in the vehicle, but he ignored me and charged straight at me, never uttering a word. I didn't have time to get to my pepper spray, so the fight was on. We wrestled on the gravel parking lot and I was eventually able to get control and put him in cuffs. Unfortunately, I found that I was completely covered in d

I started to clean myself off outside of my vehicle, but an unhappy crowd started to gather, upset with the arrest. I got into my car (oil, dirt, gravel, and all) but had to stay on scene because I had called for a tow truck to tow the suspect's vehicle. The crowd grew as I did paperwork, and the suspect's mother, who spoke absolutely no English, cried and begged me to let her son go free. It was a chaotic situation, but I had to wait for the tow truck. I left as soon as the tow truck left.

Another officer came up to me later in the shift and told me that I shouldn't say the race of the person I'm pulling over when I call in on Dispatch; it shows I'm a racist. He and I had had this conversation before, and I just agreed with him, knowing I wouldn't change his mind.

This call is a good example of why I like to give as much information out as possible when I call Dispatch during a traffic stop. When an officer makes a traffic stop, we are required to call out location, color and make of car, tag number, and number of occupants. This is mainly a safety measure. I, and many other cops, call out race and sex of the driver, if known, because we want people to have a description of the person in the event they assault us and then drive away. The officer seemed to think it made me appear biased. Frankly, I don't care what it looks like; I'd rather Dispatch have a description of my attacker when they find me dead on the side of the road. There are times when political correctness is needed, but that time ends when safety is a concern.

Chapter 8. Day Watch Diary

3/17/2011: Started on Day Watch today. I loved Morning Watch (Night Watch) but my wife never adjusted to a late shift, so being on Days will be wonderful for us. I've heard a lot of negative things about the senior sergeant. They say he's a hard boss. As long as he doesn't try to embarrass me for no reason, we'll get along fine. On the other hand, Sergeant Zastrow (not his real name) has already embarrassed me on more than one occasion so I'll have to watch him. The good thing is that my Morning Watch Supervisor also transferred to Day Watch today. He's a great guy and we get along very well.

Here's the background on what happened between me and Sergeant Zastrow: About 3 months ago I arrested a guy who was a loudmouth drunk. I brought him into the Precinct to process him. I walked him past the briefing room while Day Watch was conducting early roll-call and I guess my prisoner's yelling disturbed them. Sergeant Zastrow came to where I had the prisoner and balled me out, in front of everyone, telling me I must be "stupid" for bringing in the prisoner during roll-call. I didn't know they were having roll-call until it was too late to turn around with the prisoner, but I just sat there and let Sergeant Zastrow rant. Thirty minutes later I was writing my report with the prisoner in the report room when, unknown to me, they started late Day

Watch roll-call. Again, Sergeant Zastrow came and chewed me out for not closing the door to the report room when they started late roll-call. I wasn't looking at my watch to see when they started roll-call. He or anyone else could have closed the door. I didn't want to be alone in the room with the loudmouth drunk and the door closed because he had already said he was going to sue me and the rest of the city. I just sat and took Sergeant Zastrow's brow-beating in front of at least 10 people, including the perp. Sergeant Zastrow questioned my intellect, judgment and character.

Now, Sergeant Zastrow is one of my shift sergeants. We'll see how this goes; like Lieutenant Compost and Sergeant Willow, Sergeant Zastrow likes to make himself look good at other's expense. We'll see if he suffers the same fate as they did. What goes around comes around.

3/18: I worked Beat 207 today. Day Watch is a lot more stressful than Morning Watch. There's tons of traffic and it takes a long time to get to where you need to go. Plus, there's a lot of radio traffic and a lot of interference from management. I haven't written a traffic citation in 2 days. On Morning Watch, I averaged four to five a day. Oh well, it will get better. It sure is nice to get home and be able to do stuff. I went to the gym after work. The weather has gotten really nice so I hope to ride my motorcycle to work tomorrow.

3/19: I went to three auto accidents after noon, so ended up working 3 hours of overtime.

3/20: I went to a 2-car crash with injuries this morning. It was a horrible crash. Thankfully, no one was killed. The guy at fault was drunk at 6 o'clock in the morning. Of course, he said he only had one beer. He blew 0.129 in the breathalyzer (.08 is considered drunk).

I went to a person found deceased call; she was found dead sitting on the toilet. She was only 61 years old but had a history of taking too many opioid drugs. Very wealthy, in a $2M apartment, but it was filled with prescription drugs and liquor.

Her "best friend" came over at around 1130 and the friend was drunk. The friend wanted to hug the corpse, but the medical examiner and I said definitely not. Then, the friend started to pick up money and jewelry for "safe-keeping." Earlier, I had called the deceased's daughter, and she said the friend could speak on the daughter's behalf. However, I stopped the friend after she had about $100 and 3-4 pieces of jewelry. I told her she needed to do that with the family present. Craziness.

3/24: It's taking me a little while to get used to Day Watch. The radio is so busy and the traffic is so thick that it makes it quite hectic. Today I had a break--I was in a traffic car so I didn't have to answer 911 calls. I wrote 9 tickets but was interrupted for an hour to direct traffic because a broken-down truck closed 2 lanes.

4/22: What a day. Dispatched to theft at the Amtrak station. When I got there the Head Teller took me to the office and said a guy who they caught on video last Monday, stealing a cell phone, was back in the station. I watched the video and, sure enough, it showed him taking a phone from the Amtrak counter when he knew, or should have known, it belonged to someone else. The video showed the man look around to see if anyone was watching him, pick up the phone and hide it from view with his body, while he contemplated his crime, and then it showed him putting it in his pocket when he thought he wasn't being watched.

Amtrak had the man's identifying data, so I checked on the guy on my computer, and found he had two warrants but they were not extraditable. Nevertheless, I had probable cause to pick him up for the cell phone. He was showing "armed and dangerous" in the system, but the radio was too busy so I went it alone. I went up to the guy and asked him if he had an Android cell phone in a red case, and he said yes. So, I told him to turn around and put his hands behind his back. Before he knew what was going on, I had him in cuffs. He did indeed have the cell phone but he said he had found it. Of course, he denied all culpability.

After leaving City Property (where I put the red cell phone as evidence), I got a call about a guy who stole some stuff from a carwash. I was about 8 miles away, and the guy was reported walking up Piedmont. I went as fast as I could but was cancelled about 2 minutes out. The case was given to the beat officer, but I continued to the area and, as luck would have it, I saw the suspect at the busiest intersection in north Atlanta, Piedmont Avenue and Peachtree Road. I had to get over 4 lanes of packed traffic and across the intersection (without using my siren for fear of causing him to run) and made it to him by going against traffic with my siren for the last 100 feet. He denied knowing anything, but when I asked if I could check his stuff he said yes. As expected, he had the merchandise. As I was searching, a guy who I knew from the mini precinct last summer, Officer Armstrong (not his real name), pulled up and helped me go through the guy's bags. I didn't get the arrest because the beat officer showed up and took over.

At the end of my shift I overheard a car pursuit on my radio. I headed towards the area because they were heading my way. When I was about a half mile from them, the two robbery perps crashed and ran. A few minutes later I saw a guy matching one of the descriptions run across the road in front of me. I turned on a side road and across a train track. Knowing the guy had to eventually cross the tracks, I drove down the road next to the tracks. Sure enough, as I was slowly driving, the perp came out of the woods about 20 feet from me. I thought he would jump over my car (he was so close), but instead he fell down right at my door. I got out and jumped on him. Putting him in cuffs was easy because he was dead tired. As I was getting him up off the ground, a guy came running through the woods and it was Officer Armstrong. "Damn, you are everywhere!" he said when he saw that I had the perp.

5/1: I'm getting used to Day Watch. I've gotten 7-9 tickets each of the last 4 days. But I've only had 2-3 arrests since I came on Days.

5/12: I've made arrests four days in a row.

5/16: Had a close call today. I pulled up in front of a perp that an officer was trying to get out of a car. When the officer finally pulled the perp out, the perp's car started to roll forward into heavy traffic; he'd failed to put in Park. The officer threw the perp to the ground and ran to stop the car. The perp got up and came at the officer's back. I jumped out of my car and tackled the perp. As I was cuffing the perp, my patrol car rolled past me because I had not put it in Park. Fortunately, another officer jumped into my car and stopped it just before it hit a parked police motorcycle. Six more inches and it would have hit the motorcycle.

5/22: A Lieutenant ran roll call this morning and admonished us to increase the number of traffic citations we write. He said our numbers are down. He kidded about a conspiracy to write fewer tickets, but that is not the case at all. Morale is as good as I've seen it; the problem is that we really hit it hard last year, having a record number of citations and reducing crime in Buckhead by about 14%, and now all our good fishing places (intersections where we get a lot of violators) have dried up. Today I sat on an intersection, North Rock Springs and Piedmont, where a few weeks ago I could find a violator in about 3 minutes. Today it took 1.5 hours to get two violators. Also, all of our speed detection lasers are broken.

5/23: I went to my first DUI court cases today. DUI court is a lot tougher than regular traffic court. These defendants hire good lawyers and the process is long. My first case was easy and we won. The lawyer for my second defendant was awesome, and he wore me out like a cheap suit.

The case was a single-car accident, and when I got on scene the driver of the car was already on his way to the hospital in an ambulance. The one problem I could see with the case was that I didn't see the driver before he was taken away. But I thought I could win on that point because the firemen on scene gave me his name and DOB, the vehicle tag came back to the name when I ran it on my computer, I knew the ambulance number he was in, and he was at the hospital and drunk as a skunk when I got there. Furthermore, he identified himself to me and in his drunken state he basically admitted to the DUI without me asking. I talked to the defense attorney before the trial, and he was very friendly and said that it would be a very short trial.

As testimony started, the defense attorney had an objection for almost everything I said. He'd make an objection and cite precedents that would go on for several minutes until he wound down and the judge overruled him. This happened several times, and he cited at least ten precedents, and I started to think that the lawyer just didn't know what he was doing. Then the lawyer asked me if my written report was chronological, and I said that to the best of my ability it was. I noted some exceptions when he asked, but those exceptions were for clarity's sake. Then he asked if anything on the report was purposely out of order. I said no, but then he pointed out that on my report I wrote that I read Implied Consent (asking to give blood or breath samples) before I wrote that I arrested him. I know that I'm supposed to arrest him before I read him Implied Consent, but there it was in black and white. I never saw it coming. I even had a guy from the APD DUI Task Force read my report, and he didn't catch it. The judge threw the case out.

Was the judge's action justice? I know beyond a shadow of a doubt that the defendant was guilty. No, it wasn't justice, but it was the law. Before I left the courtroom, I got the defense lawyers card just in case I ever need a good lawyer.

5/24: I got a call to a Fight-in-Progress and was there within a minute of the call. When I arrived, there were two men struggling in a flower bed, amid a group of anti-abortion protestors. Protestors pointed the way as I drove up. The man on top of the pile was much bigger than the other guy, and he seemed to be just trying to hold the guy down.

As I approached them, the smaller guy stopped struggling and shouting. I asked the guy on top to get off and found out that the guy on bottom had seen the anti-abortion protest on his way to work and had stopped to, as he put it, "put an end to it." According to the protestors, the suspect had run up to them screaming and yelling, trying to wrestle the signs out of their hands, cursing, and threatening people that he was going to stop their protest. The protestors said the big guy, who was one of them, didn't intervene until the perp grabbed the sign of a 15-year-old girl and almost knocked her down.

The man told me on the way to jail that he was proud of what he did and would do it again. He likened himself to Martin Luther King, Jr., and Gandhi.

6/10: I went to back-up a former Academy classmate on a domestic disturbance call. When we got there, we found out that a wife walked in on her husband in bed with another woman. I think the wife had been out of town, and she surprised him with an early homecoming. The wife admitted that she had picked up a beer bottle and smashed it on the woman's face. The woman's nose appeared broken and it was bleeding profusely.

The funny thing about it was the wife wasn't upset with her husband. She talked very sweet to her husband, but every time the girl came in sight she would yell and stare her down.

About an hour before the end of shift, I got an accident call on Interstate 75. When I got on scene, there was a van behind a big commercial bus on the right shoulder. Standing behind the van was a man, and from a distance, I could see he was unsteady on his feet. I'm thinking he's drunk, but when I got up to him, I couldn't smell any alcohol.

The guy said that another car was coming into his lane, and he was distracted and rear-ended the bus in front of him. "I think the bus must have put on his brakes," he said.

The guy had all the symptoms of being drunk, but without the alcohol; he had slurred speech, droopy eyes, and he could barely stand. Of course, he failed the field sobriety test, but he didn't do as badly as the drunks I've tested in the past.

He refused a blood test, but he kept asking to take a breathalyzer. I knew the breathalyzer wouldn't give us anything. Then I got a call from a fellow officer who had some advanced DUI training, and he agreed to come out. After the officer had spent some time with the suspect, he came to me and said, "This guy is probably high on heroin or some other opiate."

I had never before dealt with a DUI that wasn't alcohol related. I looked at the suspect's eyes, and the pupils were just little spots. The suspect was upset when we got to the jail and became incensed when I took his license from him and stapled it to the ticket. "You mean I lose my license?" he slurred.

"I told you that if you refuse the blood test, you'd lose your license for a year," I replied. "If you took a blood test, you'd get a temporary permit, and you might even win the case. But by refusing, you basically are throwing away a chance to redeem yourself."

The guy seemed to be thinking hard about something, but he didn't agree to take the blood test. He probably knew that a blood test would show he was higher than a kite.

When I saw the officer later, I thanked him for his help. Without him, I really wouldn't have had much of a case. I sure wouldn't have wanted to go to court on it.

6/11: I had a Trainee today. After the academy, APD cops have to do 12 weeks of field training, so they are technically sworn officers; however, they need a little experience. (We are all one to a car here in Atlanta, so you can get in pretty deep stuff fairly quick. Experience is a must.) This trainee was fantastic! He's a big guy who speaks Spanish as well as he speaks English. And the report he wrote was perfect.

6/16: Right out of roll call, I got dispatched to back up another officer, concerning a man who walked into an apartment, took off his clothes, and got in bed with a girl. The girl screamed, and her roommates came running and chased the man off. We thought we'd be searching for a man in his underwear because the suspect left his clothes.

We found that the suspect lived in the apartment directly upstairs. It was obviously a drunken mistake, and the girls declined to prosecute, so we went up to give the guy his clothes back. The suspect's roommate answered the door and let us in, but we couldn't wake the man, so we just left the clothes next to his bed.

6/23: I went to an Injured Person call at an all-night bar, the Room Service Lounge. This was the third time I have been to this club in the last two weeks. Keep in mind, I work Day Watch and this is a "night club." Why are people still at this club at 7-o'clock in the morning? The last call was for two women being beaten up, and the call before that was for someone brandishing a gun. I talked to a cop from Zone-6 about two weeks ago, and he said that when the club was in their zone (it switched to our zone last January), they went there almost every night.

When I got on scene, another officer was already there talking to three guys in the parking lot. We asked about someone being injured, and all three acted like they didn't know what we were talking about. I went into the club and, as with every time I've been in there, I could smell the strong odor of marijuana. Naturally, no one in the club knew anything about someone being injured. The head security guy, his gold badge shining from a lanyard on his neck, said they had had no problems. I asked him about any fights outside and he said he hadn't been outside all night—great security.

"What's the deal that I have to keep coming back to this club, time after time?" I said, loudly, to no one in particular. I was hoping the owner of the club and the security people would get the message that if the violence continued, their club could be closed by the City.

"You people need to start acting like adults and going to bed at a decent hour!" I continued.

Seeing that my speech was falling on deaf ears, I ended it before I really got started.

When I went back outside, the other officer motioned toward one of the three guys she had been talking to and said that he was the guy who had called 911. I went over and started talking to the man, and it was fairly obvious that he was handicapped. He had a very pronounced stutter, limped, and his right arm was immobile. His story was that someone had pushed him down the steps, and he was really in pain. I called an ambulance.

A friend of his showed up on scene and told me that the victim had been shot in the brain several years ago, and the right side of his body was partially paralyzed. The victim gave me a description of the perpetrator, but I couldn't find anyone matching the description. Of course, no one in the club had seen anyone matching the description, and, God knows, they didn't have any surveillance cameras in the place.

I was sitting in the car filling out the report when a guy who was sweeping the club's parking lot came up to me. He was about 40 years, and very thin. He was missing several teeth, but the ones he did have gleamed bright against his dark skin. He looked like he had seen his fair share of hard times.

"What's going on, man," I said, in greeting, as he came by the car.

The man glanced around and said, "There are some very bad people in this club. I hate this place, but they pay me $100 a night to keep the place clean."

I arrested two people with warrants last time I came to the club and ran driver's licenses, so I already had an idea about the caliber of the clientele. We made small talk for a short time and then I asked, "What time does the club close?"

"Six O'clock," he said, looking around as if he were afraid someone would see us talking. "Dude, this club is owned by the mafia, and they can do just about anything they want. Hell, I got the s--t kicked out of me one night when they thought I had stolen a laptop. Wouldn't you know it; they found the damn thing a little bit later."

Later, I talked to the sergeant on duty about the club. He just kind of shrugged his shoulders, preferring to not talk about it.

7/1: I pulled over an SUV, with Alabama tags, for turning left at a crowded intersection from a Straight Only lane. The driver and his wife were obviously lost, and I initially thought that I'd let them go after giving them directions and a warning. While I was telling them why I pulled them over, the wife asked me if I knew where Legoland was.

"I didn't even know there was a Lego Land around here; sorry, I don't know where it is," I answered.

I went on to try and explain the stop to them and the wife said, "Would you hurry, we really are in a hurry, and the kids are getting restless."

I took the driver's license and wrote them a ticket for Failure to Obey Traffic Control Device. When I ran the tag on my patrol car computer, it came up as "Unknown" on the insurance tab. "Unknown" is not uncommon for out-of-state tags, and I went back to give them the ticket. As I was explaining the ticket, the wife looked at me as if to say, "I want to come over there and ring your neck." She grunted and made some exasperating noises as I asked her husband to sign the ticket. Then, I remembered the insurance status and asked to see their insurance card. The wife exploded! "Now this is just plain harassment!" she yelled, at the top of her lungs. "I work with a lot of police officers, and you guys are all alike!"

The driver took his time before signing the ticket, and then he signed on the wrong space. "No sir," I said. "Sign on the line where the X is, please."

"What difference does it make?!" he said, obviously feeling as if he shouldn't even have been stopped in the first place. I finally got the insurance card from the driver and after going back to my car--so I could read in peace--I came back to their car and returned the card.

"I'm going to be calling your supervisor on Monday!" the lady screamed. "This is pure police harassment, and you are going to pay for it!"

"Would you like to talk with him now, ma'am?" I asked.

"Hell no, I don't have the time. But I WILL report you on Monday!"

I was just thankful that every word of the exchange was caught on audio and video, because she was madder than almost anyone I've ever met. Normally my traffic stops are over in less than 10 minutes, but as I checked back in with the dispatcher, I saw that this stop had taken about 30 minutes.

When I got back to the precinct, someone explained to me where Legoland is.

Chapter 9. Complaints and Misconduct

Radio Etiquette

I got called to a single-car accident at around six a.m., and when I got there, it appeared the car had hopped a curb, run over a city sign and a few trees, and was on the median on top of some downed crepe myrtles. The driver was just getting out of the car, so I ran to help him.

The driver was unsteady on his feet, and my first thought was that he was drunk. I helped him across the busy street--amid the sounds of horns honking and passersby gathering--and called for an ambulance. Amid the noise of the street, I heard my radio blast with an alert alarm. I was still trying to figure out the driver's condition as I heard the dispatcher call my radio ID. I answered and the dispatcher said she'd been trying to raise me to see if I needed a fire engine. I yelled back over the noise that I only needed an ambulance.

After things had quieted down, and I determined the driver wasn't drunk or seriously injured, just shook up from the wreck, the sergeant called to say that the dispatcher was very upset with me. I explained the situation to the sergeant, and he suggested that I contact the dispatcher and apologize. Apologize for what? Yelling at her? It just struck me as odd that the dispatcher couldn't realize that I had my hands full, and I was yelling to be heard over the noise.

I have the utmost respect for 911 dispatchers, they have an almost impossible job and are a blessing to first responders and callers, but you would think they would be more aware of what people on the other end of the radio are going through.

Don't Make No Sense

One of my sergeants told me I had an Internal Affairs complaint, and handed me a three-page document, explaining that this was a serious complaint and needed to be investigated. In the document was a written statement from someone whom I had pulled over, several weeks earlier, for running a stoplight, and the guy was saying there was no stoplight at the intersection I pulled him over at. The complaint named about seven streets and intersections; some of the streets I didn't even recognize. The document even had pictures of street signs and intersections.

I knew something was wrong. I didn't have any recollection of these locations as part of this traffic stop, so I flipped over to the page with a copy of the citation on it. Sure enough, I had written the citation, but the intersection on the citation was not any of the intersections or streets mentioned in the citizen's complaint. The intersection on the ticket was North Rock Springs and Piedmont Avenue, which does have a light and was one of my favorite places to monitor for traffic violations.

I pointed this out to the sergeant, and you could see him relax as he realized the complaint was bogus. The sergeant said he'd handle the reply to Internal Affairs.

This kind of complaint is not uncommon. I think that many honest citizens get so upset when they get a citation, they look for anything to explain how they were not guilty, even if that means lying to themselves to the point that they truly think they are not guilty. A comparison would be when you do or say something really stupid, or out of character, and later you say to yourself, "Did I really do that? Did I really say that?"

I have had discussions with many traffic cops and, like me, they have no desire to give a ticket if it's not warranted. When I pull someone over for a traffic violation, I don't do it on a hunch, suspicion, or to fill a quota; I pull them over because I know they broke a traffic law. On the other hand, there have been a few times that I pulled someone over only to discover I was wrong (they had a Yield sign, not a Stop sign; or I was looking at the wrong light). Once I realized my mistake, I apologized and released them on their way.

I never heard any more about this particular complaint.

Just Doing My Job

One morning, I was dispatched to meet with a Night Watch officer to take over a burglary scene on Huff Road. Two businesses, Urban Plate and Interiors by Consignment, had been burglarized in a strip mall, having the glass in their front doors shattered during the night. I was assigned to secure the scene until the key holders arrived. The key holder for Urban Plate arrived around seven. By nine o'clock, there were people driving into the parking lot every few minutes, but the key holder for Interiors had not yet arrived.

At about ten minutes after nine, I was sitting in my marked patrol car when I saw a black male, about thirty-five years old with medium length dreads, standing about twenty feet to the left of my patrol car, taking pictures of the scene with a smart phone. The man was wearing a suit, but his coat was open, and I could see a gold badge hanging from his neck so I presumed he was an APD Investigator. I had not heard him check in on the radio.

As I was rolling down my car window, the man asked if there was any video of the burglary. I said that Urban Plate had video but that Interiors by Design did not. I tried to get a good look at his badge, but it was on a lanyard and hidden by his suit coat. Without identifying or introducing himself, or explaining what he was there for, he walked off towards Urban Plate.

At first, I didn't give it too much thought, but then realized I should get a solid ID of the man. He was driving a gold car, and I ran the plates, and they came back as not on record. I checked to see if the man was on the Status page of my car computer, and I couldn't find him. After about a minute or two, I followed him into Urban Plate where he was talking to two employees at the front counter. I waited a short time until there was a break in the conversation and asked him if he would show me a police ID. I didn't want to make a big deal of it, and I didn't want to interrupt the man's investigation; all I needed him to do was show me he was a cop.

The man stared at me and said nothing for a few seconds, so I repeated my request, saying something to the effect that I needed to see an ID, or at least get his name and ID number. The man blurted out a number starting with six and then said, "Outside!" pointing towards the front door.

When we got outside, the man yelled, "Don't you ever f--ing do that to me! What the f--k are you doing? Who the f--k do you think you are?"

For a brief second, I thought maybe he was working undercover and I had blown it, but quickly realized he wouldn't be talking to victims or wearing a badge if he was undercover. He said he wanted my supervisor on scene immediately, and I summoned a sergeant on Dispatch. Then the man walked to his car and I followed, half thinking he was going to jump in and drive off. He reached in the car and pulled out a police radio. When I saw the radio, and that the car was a Taurus (a commonly used unmarked car), it gave me a better feeling that he was APD, and I didn't ask any more questions. He went back inside to conduct his investigation, and I went back to my car.

It was a busy morning, and it took the sergeant about forty minutes to get on scene. The sergeant didn't say much to me after he had talked to the man. The man eventually checked in with Dispatch because his identifying data came up on my computer screen.

Later in the day, the sergeant brought me in and gave me a Letter of Counseling for lack of courtesy. On the counseling form, I saw that the man, who I then found out was Investigator Doolittle (not his real name), had told the sergeant that he had identified himself to me. At no time during the course of this event did Doolittle show me an ID, even though I asked him for it at least four times. He blurted out a number beginning with six, but didn't repeat it or give me his name when I asked.

After getting the letter of counseling, I was bummed out and woke up the next two mornings thinking, "I need to call Internal Affairs. What if Doolittle had been a perp posing as police to get hold of the video tapes? I would have been raked over the coals by the department for not positively identifying him. He lied to my sergeant, and he didn't come on the radio net until after the incident. Plus, he yelled at me like I was out of line. No, he was out of line."

I went to Internal Affairs, and after I told them my story, the Investigator said, "That turd will just come in here and lie." I guess they had dealt with Doolittle before. I never heard back from Internal Affairs about the matter.

Chapter 10. People Problems

I'm Not Googling S—t!

I pulled over a young woman going 66 in a 45-mph zone, and as I was writing her speeding citation, I noticed that she had a very wide frame around her license plate, obstructing her revalidation sticker and covering the state name. She had been cooperative when I initially approached her for the speeding, so I decided I'd just warn her about the frame.

I always like to put the good news up front when I return to a vehicle to issue citations. Furthermore, I try not to get into an involved conversation; rather, I go about my explanation whether or not they appear to be listening, have the radio up loud, are on the phone, or they're just giving me the "I Don't Care" treatment. After all, it's my responsibility to give them the information in a professional manner. It's their responsibility to listen. To do this, I have a set script that doesn't vary (unless they ask a question). I try to speak as clearly as I can, and I try to be as polite and professional as possible.

"Ma'am, I noticed that the frame around your license plate covers your revalidation sticker and most of the word Georgia. I'm not going to give you a citation for that, but state law (Georgia State Law 40-2-41) states that nothing is supposed to obstruct your license plate. I'm just warning you about that, and you should take that frame off when you can," I said.

She looked at me as if I were crazy, but I continued: "Ma'am, I'm also going to give you a break on the speed. I got you on my laser going sixty-six in a forty-five mile per hour zone, but I'm writing this citation for just fifty-nine miles per hour. That puts you in a lower speeding bracket and saves you points on your license. Sign here, please."

Instead of taking the citation, she looked away and said in a low murmur, "I'm not signing that."

"Excuse me, ma'am, what did you say?" I said as politely as possible, with hope that she'd reconsider and sign (I didn't want to do the arrest paperwork).

"I said," she said much louder and with an exasperated tone, as if she were trying to explain something to a child for the tenth time, "I'm not signing that!"

"Ma'am, if you don't sign the citation, I'll have to take you to the city jail to post bond. Signing the citation is not an admission of guilt. It just signifies that you'll pay the fine or appear in court."

She proceeded to tell me that she knew she wasn't speeding, and that I was just making up the obstructed license plate law. She finished her harangue with, "I want to see some documentation that it is a real law!"

"Ma'am, if you Google Georgia law 40-2-41...," I began, hoping to avert the necessity of taking her to jail.

"I'm not Googling s—t! Show me the law!" she insisted.

If a driver refuses to sign a citation, we are instructed to take them to jail so they can post bond. At this point, I thought about just opening the door, putting her in cuffs, and taking her to jail, but a better plan crossed my mind. "One minute, ma'am. I see that I've made a mistake on this citation," I said.

I walked back to my patrol car with her license and original speeding ticket in hand.

After a few minutes I returned to her vehicle. "Ma'am, I've corrected this ticket to reflect the correct speed, sixty-six miles per hour, twenty-one over the speed limit. Sign here, please."

She sat with her arms folded, contemplating her next move.

"Ma'am, turn off your car and hand me your keys," I said, fully intending to make her post bond.

"Okay, give me the damn ticket," she said. She hurriedly scrawled her name on the citation and handed it back as if she were doing me a favor.

"Also, ma'am, here's your documentation for the obstructed tag violation. Sign here," I said as I handed her the citation--her bona fide documentation for violating State Law 40-2-41.

She gave the signed ticket back.

I then started into my standard spiel finale: "Ma'am, these are your copies of the citations. They say the same thing that was on the ticket you signed. Again, the fine is due by the twenty-third of October," I said, as I pointed out the date to her on the ticket. "And on the back, there's a phone number and a website. You'll have to wait about a week, but after that you can call the number or go online, find out what the fine is, and pay it online or by mail. Of course, if you want to contest the ticket in court, you can do that at eight a.m. on the twenty-third. Are there any questions?"

She shouted something about seeing me in court, rolled up her window and sped off.

If a cop says the words "verbal warning," you should break out into your happy dance, because it means you're getting a break. The City of Atlanta does not give written warnings, so if someone wants documentation about a traffic law, the best I can offer is a written citation.

Mysterious Self-Moving Car

I pulled a car over for an expired tag. The female driver said, "I thought I had until the end of the month?"

"I'm sorry, ma'am, in Georgia your tag expires at midnight on your birthday," I said.

"Well, the last cop I talked to said I had until the end of the month," she replied.

I didn't argue with her. I asked her if the address on her license was correct, and she said no, that she'd moved about three years ago. Then without even pausing to get air, she said, "And I ain't changing that license until it expires in 2018 (six years away)."

In Georgia, you are supposed to get your license changed within sixty days of a change of address. I very rarely write a citation for having the wrong address on a license, and as I walked back to my car to run her license, I wasn't sure I'd write her up for the error. Before I went back to my car, I stressed that she needed to stay in her car.

The woman had led me into a small parking lot when I pulled her over, so when I returned to my patrol car, I pulled up to the side of her car (aligning my front bumper with her back door) to make room for people to drive around me in the parking lot. Also, I noticed a man videotaping the stop, probably Cop Watch, and I didn't want to be on the Cop Watch website as the poster boy for thoughtless cops.

As I was writing the ticket, the woman backed her car up about 2 feet, and I immediately got on the public address system and told her to not move her car. She yelled back that she hadn't moved it. I gave her the benefit of the doubt; maybe the car had settled when she put it into park and took her foot off the brake.

Then, the woman got out of the car and shouted that she wanted my name and badge number. I instructed her to get back in her car, and I assured her that she'd get all that information when I returned to her car.

I resumed writing the ticket and was interrupted by a radio call telling me to call such-and-such phone number. I wrote down the number and called. An Atlanta Police Officer, Officer Smith, identified himself, but I didn't know him. Smith said that the girl I had just pulled over was his ex-girlfriend, and she was an "entertainer" (exotic dancer) and had been out of town, and that was why she hadn't gotten her car registered. Smith asked me to give her a break and not write her a ticket.

"Well, she told me that she thought she didn't have to get it registered until the end of the month," I told him. There was silence for a few seconds, then I said, "I'm sorry, but this woman has given me nothing but a hard time; she's getting these tickets." Again, a long pause on the phone, then the line went dead.

I realized that Smith was probably the cop who had given her the wrong information about her registration. Sealing my decision to also write the ticket for not updating the address on her license, the woman moved the car again, about 4 feet forward. I guess that was her way of displaying her displeasure with the traffic stop.

When I went back to the woman, she was just as sweet as could be. All I could figure was that Officer Smith had told her to not press her luck with me. He probably told her that he'd fix the tickets later (more bad news; it's virtually impossible for an APD officer, not involved in a case, to get a ticket rescinded or "fixed.").

"Ma'am, I'm sorry it took so long, but I had to take a phone call while I was writing your citations," I said when I returned to issue her the citations.

Later, I was talking to a female cop about the stop, and she said, "Ex? That ain't no ex! That's probably Smith's hook-up, and he doesn't want anyone to know. Who in the hell goes to bat for an Ex!"

Hard to argue with her logic.

Merry Christmas!

On a Christmas morning, around nine o'clock, I pulled a guy over for going sixty mph in a forty-mph zone. He seemed fine when I initially talked with him, but when I returned with the citation, he went ballistic. His main beef was that I had already pulled out the yellow copy (driver's copy) when I gave him the ticket to sign. "This is highly irregular bull-s#!t!" he said, and proceeded to tell me he was going to call my supervisor.

He repeatedly asked for my badge number (which I gave him at least twice) and continued complaining as I tried to explain to him that I didn't need the signature on the driver's copy; he was keeping the driver's copy and didn't need his own signature on it. Also, he wasn't listening as I tried to tell him I was reducing his ticket to fifty-four mph so that he would only be fourteen mph over the limit. This would save him a lot of money and wouldn't put points on his license. As he ranted, I had a change of heart and interrupted him, saying, "Oh, you're right! It looks like I made a mistake on this ticket."

I went back to my car and changed the fifty-four to a sixty. The man didn't say anything about the change and continued to rant, adding a sarcastic, "Merry Christmas," as he signed the citation.

As he started to drive away, he yelled out the window, "Oh yeah, you're probably a Jew, giving tickets on Christmas. Happy Hanukkah, Jew!"

As he drove off, the only thing I could think of to reply with was, "Mazel Tov!"

I've Got to Pee

I pulled in behind a car with a drive-out tag that said, "Test Drive." I had to take a pee, so I was happy to see the car turn into a store parking lot. I continued on, intending to overlook the tag and get to a restroom, but saw the car pull back out onto the road in my rearview mirror. The car was in the right lane, going the same direction as me, with its right blinker on. I was in the left lane, waiting to turn left at a light. When the light turned green, I waited for the car to pass me on the right. But the car didn't move, and I could see in my side view mirror that the car had changed its blinker to a left turn. After a few seconds, the car's horn honked, so I went ahead and made my left turn, thinking the car would also turn left behind me. However, the car turned right, so I activated my lights, cut a U-turn, and pulled up behind it. The car continued for about 300 yards, as I followed with lights and siren, before pulling over.

As soon as I approached, the driver told me that she was lost. I got her license, and it showed that she lived in the area. I then started to tell her why I had pulled her over, but she interrupted to say she was on her way to the Department of Motor Vehicles to get her tag. She showed me a traffic citation that she had gotten a week earlier for not having a tag. She swore to me, several times, that she was on her way to the Department of Motor Vehicles "at this very minute!"

As the lady talked, her ten-year-old son, sitting in the front passenger seat, kept making faces and sticking his tongue out at me. The lady showed me a bill-of-sale, so she wasn't on a "test drive." When I asked to see her emissions inspection (required to get a car registered in Atlanta), she said that she was going to get it after she got the tag. I tried to explain to her that she had to have the inspection prior to getting a tag, but she just kept on making up excuses; "I was sick…I didn't have the money…I was going to get it today."

Normally, I would have just given her a ticket for no tag. But the lies (and the kid sticking out his tongue) convinced me that she needed a little extra incentive. I cited the lady for no tag, improper signaling, and for using a tag to conceal the identity of her vehicle. In addition, I impounded the car.

The lady called 911 while I was talking to her and told them I was holding her against her will and taking her car. She also asked for my supervisor.

Oh, the joys of police work. "Now, where's that bathroom?"

Training the Untrainable

One of my trainee's, Officer Victor (not her real name), seemed to have a problem accepting instruction and constructive criticism. On my first day with her, I changed a call, that she had classified as a Hit-and-Run accident, to a Damage to Property offense, because we had no proof that the damaged vehicle was hit by another vehicle--we had damage, but no way of verifying it was caused by someone else in a vehicle. If we had a witness, video of the accident, vehicle debris in the road, we could reasonably conclude that it was a hit-and-run accident. However, by just going on the basis of the vehicle owner's word, we could possibly be assigning blame to the wrong person. For all we knew, the "Victim" (vehicle owner) could have hit something at an earlier time and was now getting an accident report to cover up the facts. Officer Victor just couldn't see my rationale for changing the classification. As I tried to explain, she stared off into space, didn't respond that she understood, and shook her head side-to-side.

Whether or not Officer Victor liked it, I changed the call from Hit-and-Run (an accident) to Damage to Property (an offense).

For clarification, in an accident report, the vehicle operator(s) (sometimes it's the owner) are classified as Drivers; in an Offense report people are classified as either Suspects, Victims, Witnesses, Arrestees, or Reporting Parties; they are never classified as Drivers. However, Officer Victor insisted that the Victim in this offense should be classified as a Driver. After about ten minutes of explaining, I finally ordered her to classify the driver as a Victim. She didn't like it, but I assured her she could take it to a supervisor later and really show them how "dumb" I was.

I didn't think too much of it at the time because she ended up writing a good report, and it was just our first day together.

Three days later, I got a similar reaction from her when I tried to explain that we needed to narrow down the timeframe of three Thefts from Auto (that occurred on the same block, on the same night, and with the same M.O.). As I tried to explain the timeframe, she didn't make eye contact, didn't respond verbally, and just shook her head. I tried to explain it to her in different ways; she couldn't follow my logic.

After each of these incidents, she gave me the silent treatment for several hours, only answering my questions with short responses, often just turning her head towards me and not responding verbally. I think turning her head towards me was her way of saying, "I can hear you, but you're an idiot, and I'm not listening." Because she seemed very book-smart, I gave her passing marks and determined to just continue to stay positive with her, hoping she'd eventually realize there was a good reason behind these decisions.

Throughout this time, she repeatedly wrote my last name wrong (putting an "s" at the end), followed other vehicles too closely, and made other mistakes that seemed to be intentional. She was, supposedly, a Spellman College graduate, so I was having a hard time figuring out why she couldn't, or wouldn't, follow instructions.

The next day, towards the end of the shift, I had already filled out Officer Victor's grade book when we got a credit card theft call. During that investigation, Officer Victor was interviewing a woman who had her credit cards taken by a couple of guys who had stayed overnight with her and her roommate. The victim's story sounded suspicious to me because the woman denied having a romantic relationship with the any of the suspects even though they had slept together the night before; she slept with one suspect and her roommate with the other. When Officer Victor paused in her interview, I took the time to ask the victim how well she knew the suspects and questioned the victim's relationship to the suspect she'd slept with. As I was questioning the women, Officer Victor apparently felt I was interfering with her investigation and physically moved between the woman and me, starting a new line of questioning.

I let Victor continue, but when she gave the two women business cards, with contact and case information, I noticed that she had, once again, added an "s" to the end of my name on both cards. Officer Victor told me she was done with her investigation, so I instructed her to go to the patrol car. I stayed and got the real story from the women; they did know the suspects' names, they knew where one of them lived, and, yes, they had regular contact and intimacy with the suspects.

Officer Victor and I didn't talk on the ride back to the precinct, but once there, as an opening to mend our fragmented relationship, I told her that I thought the women's story was only half true, and that's why I had intervened with my questions. Officer Victor explained that she was the same age as the women and that their story made perfect sense to her. I reminded Victor that she was in training, and she needed to take my lead when I felt it necessary to contribute to an investigation. I changed the grade for "Takes Instruction" in Officer Victor's grade book. Officer Victor made it very clear to me that she didn't agree with my changes. She also told me that her boyfriend, an APD Motorcycle cop, had told her that I was wrong, and she was right. Her protests did not improve her failing grade.

Officer Victor immediately went from our patrol car to the Sergeant's office and complained about me. Fortunately, the sergeant took my side. It helped that I had all of her behavior on patrol car camera.

Officer Victor's behavior improved over the next few days, and I was optimistic I could make a police officer out of her. However, in addition to her problem with authority, Officer Victor apparently had a courage deficit.

One morning, while it was still dark, we spotted a parked car that matched the description of one which an armed robber was driving. When I went up to confirm the vehicle identification number (VIN), I saw that there was someone sleeping in the car. After writing down the last five digits of the VIN, I looked at the guy with a flashlight but wasn't sure if he matched our suspect. I motioned for Victor to come and verify my findings; however, she froze. I had to walk back to her and insist she take a look at the suspect. She very slowly tiptoed to the suspect and shined her light on him for less than a second before running back to me and saying he wasn't our suspect.

I looked up the suspect's photo again on the computer and thought Officer Victor might redeem herself by taking another trip to check out the suspect more thoroughly. She just sat there, arms folded and shaking her head. Eventually, I went back to make sure the guy sleeping in the car wasn't the suspect. He wasn't.

The remainder of the day, Officer Victor and I got along well up until I filled out her grade book. When she saw that I had given her some low grades, she fell back into her passive aggressive ways. At the end of the shift, I made it clear to her that her grades were nothing personal; they were a direct reflection of her performance. She wasn't happy.

I don't know what became of Officer Victor, but she never completed field training.

I had about seventy Trainee's during my time with the Atlanta Police Department. Only two of them didn't complete field training. Officer Victor was one of them. The other refused to help me clear a house that supposedly had a burglar in it. Some people are just not cut out for this job.

Chapter 11. Shut-up!

If in Doubt, Say Nothing

During a traffic stop, I discovered that the driver's license showed she weighed 170 pounds, but, to me, she didn't look as if she weighed more than 110. I made the mistake of saying she didn't look like she weighed 170 pounds and maybe she should consider getting her license renewed. She went ballistic. I never got a chance to explain myself because she wouldn't stop yelling.

She called the precinct within minutes, and I had to explain the situation to my sergeant; I had meant the comment as a compliment. Luckily, the sergeant understood my mistake, and the lady didn't press for a further investigation.

When I told my wife about the incident, she reminded me that I should never mention a woman's weight to her, even if it's intended as a compliment.

I should have known better; I've been married over 30 years and have two adult daughters. Oh well, live and learn, over-and-over-and-over.

In contrast, I've had many instances where the driver's license said a person weighed such-and-such, but over just a few years they had apparently gained 100 or more pounds. I see that kind of weight discrepancy every week. It makes me wonder how people can gain so much weight in just a few years.

Appearances Are Deceiving

I pulled a lady over for running a stop sign. When I looked at her license, it said she was 5'-04" and weighed eighty-five pounds. I had talked to her several minutes, and she sure appeared a lot heavier than eighty-five. If I had to guess, I'd say she was close to 175 pounds. When I went back to her car and started to give her a ticket, she said that she was paraplegic and had to control the car with her hands only. I looked down and saw that her legs were very thin. That probably accounted for her light weight.

She showed me how her car was modified for a hand-braking system and explained that it was harder to bring the car to a stop with a handbrake.

In case you're wondering; yes, I gave her the citation.

Big Mouth

One day in December I noticed a cloud of thick smoke coming from a few blocks away. I drove around the neighborhood, towards the smoke, and came upon a house set off the road about 100 feet. It was hard to tell if the smoke was coming from the backyard or from the house itself, so I parked my patrol car. I found an unattended pile of leaves burning in the backyard.

A man came to the door when I knocked. The man said he thought Georgia law allowed you to burn leaves in the wintertime. I explained to him that Georgia Law allowed it, but that a city ordinance prohibited it.

Then, a female voice from inside the house shouted, "That's just bulls#!t! That's all you cops know how to do, bother folks!"

The lady came to the door and proceeded to go on a tirade about the police. I tried to sympathize with her, being a huge fan of leaf burning myself. I finally got her to calm down by assuring her that I wasn't there to arrest anyone for burning leaves, or even give a ticket. In fact, I agreed that putting out the fire would be very difficult, and I just wanted them to tend the fire and not do anymore burning.

She seemed satisfied with the turn of events, and as I was leaving, I asked for her name and date of birth, for my records.

I ran her on my patrol car computer and discovered she had a warrant for Domestic Battery.

She was not very happy to find herself sitting in the back of my patrol car.

Show Me in Writing

A fellow officer told me a humorous story. He said he saw a man walking his dog, and after the dog took a large crap on the grass by the sidewalk, the man didn't pick it up. As the man walked by, my friend said, "Hey, aren't you going to clean up after your dog?"

"I don't have a bag. I'll have to go back home and get one," the man said, somewhat sarcastically.

My friend told the man that he needed to carry a bag with him when he walked his dog. My friend said he didn't have any intention of giving the man a citation until the man replied, "Is it some sort of law?"

"It's a City ordinance," my friend said.

"Oh yeah?" said the man. "Show it to me in writing!"

My friend said that he showed the man in writing, on the citation he gave him.

It does my heart good to know that police officers will go the extra mile to help a citizen understand the law.

Chapter 12. Angels Watching Over Us

A Still Small Voice

On a Sunday morning, I pulled over a car I had paced at sixteen mph over the speed limit. Before I even got to the driver's back bumper, I knew I wasn't going to write the person a ticket. It was as if, when the driver rolled down the window, angels came out and said, "Don't give this person a ticket, she's protected."

I believe in angels, but I'm not the kind of person who spiritualizes a lot of things. I didn't see angels, and probably didn't actually hear any speak, but there was an almost audible voice talking to me.

"Oh, I'm so sorry officer. I'm a little late for church, but I'm not that late," the older woman behind the wheel said after I explained the reason for the traffic stop to her.

I went through the motions of the stop, and back at the patrol car, my trainee must have thought I was sick or something because all I said to him, after he checked her license on the patrol car computer, was, "We ain't giving this lady a ticket."

In fact, we didn't give a ticket the rest of the day.

In those days, I gave at least three citations a shift. I had given eleven citations the day before and was used to giving, on average, five a day. That day was only the second day since I hit the streets, two years earlier, that I purposely didn't give out a citation.

The Voice Returns

I pulled a guy over for speeding and when I asked for his license, he started patting his pockets, a good sign that he probably didn't have one. I got a very weird feeling, and I unlocked my holster and secretly pulled my gun, hiding it behind my back. I had a fleeting thought that if someone reviewed my patrol car video, they'd probably wonder why I was pulling my gun; it was just a traffic stop in the middle of the day, but I just had a sneaking suspicion that this guy was dangerous. Again, it was as if a voice told me to do it.

The man started to look for his license in a bag that was on the passenger seat but, again, something told me not to let him into that bag. I told him to just give me his name and birth date.

I went back to the car and ran the driver on my computer, and the alert sounded, letting me know there was something wrong with the license (i.e., warrants, expired, suspended, etc.).

Without even checking to see what the discrepancy was, I went back and put the guy in cuffs. I told him he wasn't under arrest but was being detained until I could finish my investigation. When I searched him, as part of the detention, I found his license in his pocket. The guy eventually came clean and admitted that he had given me his brother's name and date of birth because he had some warrants.

When I checked the man on my computer, using his real name and date of birth, he had warrants for aggravated assault, battery, and several failure-to-appear (FTA) warrants. As I was inventorying the contents of the car, I found a loaded 9mm pistol in the bag on the passenger seat. I broke out in a cold sweat when I recalled that he tried to go into this bag when he was looking for his license. I unloaded his gun, making sure my car camera caught everything. Later, I asked the guy if he had thought about pulling out the gun when I pulled him over.

"To be honest," he said, "it crossed my mind. But I'm not that kind of guy."

Not that kind of guy? I didn't say it, but his warrants showed he was "that kind of guy!"

Out of curiosity, I checked the info under his brother's name and found that the brother had an FTA for traffic, and that was why I got the alert. The Lord was really looking out for me, because he very likely would have pulled out his weapon. In addition, I probably would have taken him for his brother if the alert hadn't sounded, and I wouldn't have found out who he really was.

Chapter 13. It Takes All Kinds

I Know Stuff

I pulled over a guy for speeding, and he really pulled out all the stops to get out of his ticket. As I approached the car, he opened the door and started to get out, holding out his hand and smiling as if we were old friends. I told him to stay in the car. Initially he said that he wasn't speeding, but after I told him I visually estimated his speed at sixty before confirming it with my laser, he smiled and said he was sorry to put me "to all this trouble," but his car was a rental and he was sure the speedometer was broken. "I think it's reading slow because it said I was only doing forty-five."

He proceeded to tell me that he was a retired school Principal and had a lot of cop friends. "Do you know Major Smith?"

Without answering him, I told him to stay in the car. As I was writing the citation, I could see him talking animatedly on his phone.

"I bet you he's talking to a cop," I said to my Trainee.

"How do you know?"

"I know stuff," I said, half-jokingly.

When I went back to give the driver his citation, he continued to plead his innocence--I had to tell him three times to sign on the line with the X. He made a big deal about how foolish I'd feel when he showed the judge that his speedometer was broken. As I was leaving, he ended his argument with a loud, "Have a blessed day!"; emphasizing the word "blessed."

About an hour later, I got a phone call from a sergeant, asking me if I had given a ticket to a Mr. So-and-so. The sergeant then gave me a phone number so I could call a retired APD Major Smith. My Trainee looked at me with astonishment as he overheard my phone conversation, saying, "You do know stuff. He was talking to a cop."

I never called retired Major Smith.

Be Careful What You Ask For

I pulled a very nice Audi sedan over for not stopping at a stop sign. After I approached and positioned myself just behind the window post, the man inside slowly lowered the window, as if he didn't want to be bothered, continued his conversation on his Bluetooth, and just looked ahead as if I wasn't there? Once he finished his phone conversation, I explained why I had pulled him over. He grudgingly nodded his head.

When I was back at my patrol car, writing the citation, I noticed that the frame around his license plate was covering most of the revalidation sticker and the name of the State. I thought about giving him a citation for the tag but decided against it because I hadn't mentioned it to him during my initial approach.

After he signed the citation for the stop sign, I gave him a verbal warning about the frame. He became incensed, saying, "That's bullshit! You show me the law that says I can't have a frame around my license plate...."

When he finished his monologue, I asked him to stay in the car, and went back and wrote him a citation for the frame. I figured he'd really blow his top when I came back with the additional citation, but the guy took the second citation with no complaint. Now, why couldn't he have been that nice earlier in the encounter?

I write this story not to show how much I enjoy giving tickets to jerks (which I do), but because I want to stress the importance of treating officers with respect. Police have the most thankless job in the world and get paid peanuts for it. I've had at least thirty occasions where citizens told me they were going to send a commendation about my good customer service to the Chief. How many did I get? None. In my opinion, what I did as a police officer was a hundred times more beneficial to society than what I did in the Air Force, and I was paid more than twice as much in the Air Force. So, the next time you encounter a cop, treat them with some dignity. That cop is probably a great person and proud to serve the community. Also, the odds of you getting a ticket are much less if you show some courtesy. Act like a jerk, and you're sure to get that well-deserved ticket.

Rock and Roll

About forty-five minutes before the end of my shift, I got called to a woman who wanted to file a report because she'd gotten a flat tire. As I approached the scene, I could see the lady standing in the road next to her car, yelling and pointing at guys poring cement from a cement mixer truck onto a driveway. When she saw me, she dropped her hands and forced a smile.

The lady told me she had run over a piece of concrete that had come from the truck. She wanted me to make the truck company compensate her for her flat tire.

I talked to the workers, and they showed me where they had a flagman and signs installed showing men at work, and how they had blocked off part of the lane to keep people from driving in that area. They even showed me their City permit to shut down one lane of the road.

"The problem is, this lady, after being flagged through, flew down this stretch of road like she was mad she'd had to wait, totally ignoring the debris," one of the men said.

I surveyed the construction workers' traffic setup, and the size of the concrete rock the woman claimed gave her the flat tire, and determined that the workers had used reasonable care, and the lady probably didn't use reasonable care. In addition, it appeared the lady had plenty of room to miss the concrete if she were going the speed limit and paying attention to the road.

I explained to the lady that no crime had been committed; however, I would do a Damage to Property report for her.

This was the second time in as many weeks that I had someone wanting a police report for a flat tire. I wouldn't even think of calling the police for a flat tire; it's just part of driving. I know the police are here to serve, but flat tires aren't criminal. What's next, reports for dental cavities? Flat tire reports are a waste of police time unless the tire is flattened maliciously or the City of Atlanta is somehow at fault. In any case, this was a civil issue, not a criminal issue.

I got all the information from the lady, and she assured me that she was telling the truth: she had been driving on the city street, ran over the concrete and flattened her tire, and it had happened just before I arrived. She said she had parked the car where it currently was, on the street, with a flat tire.

I asked the woman for her license, but she said she had left it at home. I got her identifying information (i.e., name, date of birth, height, etc.) and ran her name through the computer. I filled out a report form, stating the report number and who to contact in order to get a copy of the report for her records. After handing her the report form, I also gave her two citations; one for No License on Person (because she was driving without a license on her person) and another for Driving with An Expired License. Unbeknown to her, her license had expired two days earlier.

This is a perfect example of being careful what you ask for. In this case, if she hadn't berated the workers, they probably would have changed her tire for her, just to help her out. However, by insisting on "justice," she failed to take into account her own possible wrongdoing. Remember, when you call the police, they are on the law's side, not necessarily on your side.

Funky-Smelling Car

I pulled a lady over for having an expired tag. When she rolled the window down, the funky smell of body odor, bad breath, feces, and cigarettes rolled out of the car like fog. There was a little girl in the front passenger seat, and the lady told me the girl was five years old (minimum age to not be in a child seat is seven years.). The lady resented being pulled over and started to drop names of people she knew on the police force and in City government.

I ticketed her for the registration and not having the child in a child's seat. I also gave her a ticket for obstructed tag, because the frame around the tag covered the expiration sticker.

While I was writing the tickets, the driver got out and walked back to tell me the car's owner wanted to talk to me on the phone. The driver was a twenty-something-year-old adult, so I told her to get back in the car; I didn't need to talk to the owner.

When I got back to the precinct, an officer said that the funky-smelling car I had pulled over belonged to a police officer who was undergoing cancer treatment and wanted me to call the officer. I felt bad for a moment but didn't call the officer back (I didn't impound the car, so the officer was not liable for anything.). The driver earned every citation.

Miranda is a Friend of Mine

I had a guy tell me he wasn't going to sign his traffic ticket without his lawyer present. On impulse, I started reading him his Miranda Rights. When he asked me why I was reading him his rights, I said, "Well, I want you to have your lawyer, so I'm going to arrest you and let you meet him at jail." He signed.

Chapter 14. Surviving a Traffic Stop

The president of the men's group at my church asked me to speak at the monthly men's meeting. He said that the topic was up to me. At first, I was leaning toward some sort of devotion or lesson that would be a spiritual inspiration to the men. After some thought, I came to the conclusion that a Bible lesson would probably bore them; most of these guys work all day, and they needed something to keep them awake following the fellowship dinner, which always preceded the meeting. I concluded that my area of expertise, if I had one, was policing. I decided to give them a short lesson on how to avoid being stopped by the cops, and what to do to mitigate the damage if they were stopped. Want to hear it? Here it go:

Speech to Church Men's Group

I can only speak for myself (I'm sure the Atlanta Police Department is happy about that), but most cops are not going to pull you over for going less than 10 miles over the speed limit. I only use under 10 miles over when I'm running laser in school zones or on a narrow road where there is a history of accidents. Generally, I use 15 miles over as my threshold. On my beat, there is one road where I use 21 miles per hour over before I pull someone over for speeding. And on the highways around Atlanta, if you aren't going at or over the speed limit, FORGETABOUTIT! However, by all means keep your speed within 10 miles of the limit; you should be okay.

Another area where motorists can keep themselves out of trouble with the law is to obey signs at intersections. It's easy picking for a cop to sit and watch people run lights and signs. So, pay special attention to signs that say No Right on Red, No U-turn and come to a full stop at stop signs.

These tips, and others, will not only prevent trouble with the law, but they will prevent injury, damage, and the headaches that come with dealing with guys like me and the justice system. Everyone pays for an accident. If you don't believe that, just do a computer search of accident rates and their effect on motor vehicle insurance and taxes.

During my first two days on my new beat, in the western part of the city, there were three bad accidents at the same intersection. There was extensive damage and airbag deployment in all the accidents. In two cases, cars ended up off the road, and one came to rest upside-down. And there was a fatality in one case. In all the accidents, the person at fault had turned right on a red light without first coming to a stop and checking for traffic. This right on red after stopping law is found in all 50 states, and it should be common sense.

However, if there's one thing I've learned as a police officer, it is: common sense is not all that common.

There's an empty lot, used for overflow parking by a local business, close to this particular intersection, so I started sitting in the lot and monitoring traffic. It was a traffic cop's dream come true. So many people ran that light, I could write as many tickets as time allowed. Virtually 90% of the cars never came to a complete stop before turning. If I pulled them all over, I wouldn't have had time to answer calls on my beat, so I only pulled the most egregious cases over; those cars that not only didn't stop but only slowed down enough to make the turn.

There was not another accident, during my shift, at that intersection for the next four months, and for the next year and a half there were only two, both of which were minor. Furthermore, I averaged about two accidents a week during the first month I was on that beat, but that dropped to about one every other week as I aggressively pursued my traffic duties. My conclusion is that motorists saw my flashing blue lights so often, they slowed for fear there were other cops in the area. An added benefit was that all crime in that area fell dramatically. Again, I was so visible, the perps probably thought there were more cops hiding, waiting to pounce.

Despite the best of intentions, most motorists will eventually be pulled over by a cop. My instruction to you is, don't panic. Cops are human, and they make mistakes too. My five speeding violations are testament to that. Also, despite what you hear, the vast majority of cops (I'm sure it's in the 99th percentile) don't pull people over for quotas, or because they don't like the color of their skin. Heck, on most stops I don't know the race or sex of the driver until I'm stopped behind them with lights flashing. This is especially true in the south where most people have tinted windows.

(At this point I told the men that there are some do's and don'ts that may help them get out of a ticket, or at least reduce the type and amount of tickets they get.)

If you are pulled over, don't just stop in the middle of the street. The biggest danger for law enforcement is getting hit by traffic. (As I write this, I am reminded that the last three on-duty fatalities in the Atlanta Police Department were a result of officers being hit by vehicles.) Pull over to the side of the road, or pull off at the next road if it is less busy. Also, don't keep driving so that you can pull over in a busy parking lot. Generally, I don't put my blue flashers on until I'm in a good area for the stop. Sometimes that may be an empty lot. However, I get very wary when I'm in a busy parking lot, because there is a lot of traffic coming towards me from all directions. At least when I pull someone over on the side of the street, I only have to worry about traffic and people approaching from one direction. In a parking lot, I also have to be concerned about pedestrians approaching me as I conduct a stop. There are many cases of cops being confronted by an upset citizen or, worse yet, a homicidal maniac, as they undertake a traffic stop.

(The presentation concluded with questions and answers.)

Chapter 15. The Rest of the Story

Mr. Reynolds Returns

I walked into work one morning and heard a deep, resonant, baritone voice, that I immediately recognized, coming from the suspect holding room. Sure enough, when I looked in the room, I saw a guy I had arrested over a year earlier, Mr. Reynolds; the man who had eaten for free at Cheesecake Factory. He was explaining to a group of three young officers how he hadn't kidnapped a girl, rather, she had insisted on going with him, and when he asked her to leave, she wouldn't. As I listened, I could tell that Mr. Reynolds was trying to spin another lie to get himself out of a jam.

His story was quite fascinating, and he had everyone in the room paying close attention. However, I couldn't resist, saying, "I arrested that guy a year ago for not paying his bill at Cheesecake Factory."

Mr. Reynolds tried to appear indignant, and said, "Are you saying I'm lying?"

"Are your lips moving?" I responded.

The room went quiet as the cops realized that probably everything Mr. Reynolds had been telling them was a lie. We all left within a few seconds, leaving Reynolds alone to ponder his future.

Lt. Compost, Sgt. Willow, and Sgt. Zastrow (not their real names)

About a year after I joined the force, Sergeant Willow was fired from the force and a month after that I learned that Lieutenant Compost had also been fired. I don't know if they got their pensions or not, but they sure lost money and their reputations.

The story I heard is that Sergeant Willow was working an extra job when a dead body was found. Apparently, she was supposed to handle the case, but she pushed the investigation off on World Congress Center Police. I was told when Internal Affairs asked her about it, she denied any knowledge of the case. However, her name was in the WCC Police report, so she was caught lying.

As for Lieutenant Compost, I heard that he was claiming to be at work when in reality he wasn't. Bottom line for both of them is that they got caught in a lie. I had always wondered why they constantly thought we, the officers, were not telling the truth. Now, I had my answer; they expected us to be lying just like them.

On the other hand, I came to really like and respect Sergeant Zastrow. He was a real go-getter, very competent, and a very nice person once you got to know him. Like me, he had a strange sense of humor. He eventually made lieutenant, and I was sad when he retired a couple of years after that.

Beat 203

After about five years as a street cop and over three years in Beat 203, I found myself very confident in my abilities. So far, I hadn't had to shoot anybody and nobody had shot me. I'd been in more than a few fights but had come through them all with only minor scrapes. I had made several great connections in the zone and knew my beat well. I'd been successful in driving most of the prostitutes off my beat and brought the number of burglaries down. I had led the watch in enforcement, averaging around nine hundred citations and ninety arrests a year. In addition, I had seen crime on my beat reduced by about two-thirds. Unfortunately, the criminals in Zone-1, just south of 203, had discovered that 203 was easy pickings during Night Watch, and started having nightly vehicle break-in parties. They'd go into a darkened parking lot and hit several cars and be gone in a matter of a few minutes. I spent a lot of my mornings, during my last year in 203, investigating thefts from automobiles.

In spite of this setback, I was very proud of what I had accomplished. In the first week of being on the beat, we'd had three very serious accidents at the intersection of Chattahoochee Avenue and Marietta Boulevard. All of the accidents had sent people to hospital, and in one case a person was killed. In addition, someone had been beaten to death with a hammer at that intersection. In that case, the victim had gone into a bank to get cash, and when he came back to his van, two men, unbeknownst to him, had hidden in the back, not revealing themselves until after he had driven off. Apparently, he put up a fight, and the suspects ended up beating him to death with one of his own hammers.

To curtail accidents, I started posting myself at that intersection whenever I had time and discovered that people rarely stopped on Chattahoochee before turning right when the light was red. In fact, many people barely slowed down before pulling out onto Marietta Boulevard. I saw several near-misses.

This was a very dangerous situation, because people often sped, twenty to thirty miles over the limit, on Marietta Boulevard--it was a wide road with good turning lanes, and people got the impression that it was wide open for speed. I started pulling people over for running the light and was racking up five, sometimes up to ten citations a day. Keep in mind, I didn't pull people over if they slowed and used some caution. I only pulled the ones who, in my estimation, slowed down just enough to make the turn. I had a great vantage point from a parking lot, and people didn't even know I was in the area. After a year of doing this, I realized that there had not been another serious accident at the intersection. In fact, there were no serious accidents there for my entire time in 203, and after the first two years, I rarely staked out the intersection; people were cautious because they assumed I was nearby.

When I first arrived on 203, I noticed that there were a lot of women just walking around, seemingly doing nothing. Not being fully street-wise, I initially didn't think much of this. But after a few weeks, I had a case where one of the women said she was robbed by one of her "Johns."

"Johns?" I asked.

"Yeah, the dude wanted to f--k me in the butt, but I said he'd have to pay first," she answered. "He got mad, grabbed my purse, and drove off."

"Oh, his name's not John, he is a 'John,'" was my thought as a not-so-bright lightbulb went off in my head.

I combatted prostitution by being visible. I started by just driving in the areas where prostitutes most frequently walked. Sometimes I'd park and talk to them as they went by my car. They were usually friendly.

"Hey, what you up to?" I'd ask, as friendly as I could.

"Oh, I'm just taking a walk," or, "I'm just chillin'," they'd say.

After a while, I got to know some of their names, and one day I was talking to one of the women at a gas station convenience store when the conversation came around to Zodiac signs.

"What's your sign, Officer Duke?" she asked.

"I'm a Scorpio, born on October twenty-ninth," I answered. That's not my real birthdate, but it was a Zodiac day I knew, because I had dated a girl in high school who was a Zodiac adherent and often referred to her birthdate.

"Damn! I'm a Sagittarius, born on November twenty-ninth," she said, smiling and raising her voice in excitement. "I think you and I could get along," she continued, obviously warming up to the idea that we had some sort of connection.

"What year?" I asked, as if I was just as excited about our connection as she was.

"Nineteen Eighty-eight," she said proudly.

After a little more small-talk, I hurried to my patrol car and ran her information on my Mobile Data Terminal (MDT). BINGO! She had a warrant for failing to go (FTA) to court.

I noticed that the woman had walked down the street, so I headed that way and pulled up right next to her. She met me with a big smile, "What's up, Officer Duke?"

I smiled back and said, "I have some bad news for you…"

It only took about two months before I saw the number of women walking the street on my shift fall to just a few. With the reduction, I found that the number of calls for assaults, domestic arguments, trespassing, and shoplifting fell dramatically.

After about four months, I was left with just one prostitute, Nancy.

Nancy looked to be about sixty-five to seventy years old, thin as a rail and toothless. I later found that she was only in her forties; that just shows you what hard living and crack cocaine can do to you. Incidentally, she was the only white prostitute I knew of on the beat.

For a while, I thought she was a homeless person, never imagining this wrinkled, toothless, shabby person would be a desirable sex object. One day I saw her lying in the middle of a parking lot at an intersection, in full view of two main streets, with her knees up, dress fallen back to her waist, and her lady parts showing--not a stitch of underwear.

I drove up and approached her top half (head), not wanting a closeup of anything that might haunt me for the rest of my life. She was asleep. I woke her up, helped her get her things together and get out of there, then spent the rest of the shift trying to wash the picture of her laying there, in all her glory, out of my mind.

Through my connections with residents and shop owners, I learned that people actually paid Nancy for sexual favors.

I arrested Nancy at least four times, mostly for trespassing, but she was still around when I left the beat years later. She's probably still there if she's still alive.

As a white person, I was in the minority on Beat 203; however, there was a neighborhood off Bolton Road which was mostly white. I referred to it as my Meth Den, because methamphetamine was the drug of choice.

Apparently, many of the meth-heads thought that I would go easy on them because I was white.

'We've never had a white officer here before, it's about time,' was one of the common comments I got from them.

I started to cultivate some friendships on the beat, with blacks, Hispanics, and whites, but it was the whites that would go out of their way to say hello or shoot the breeze. That was about to change.

One afternoon, about two months after coming to Beat 203, I pulled over a car for speeding. I didn't know who I had pulled over; all I knew was that he was doing about twenty miles per hour over the speed limit. It is rare for a traffic officer to know who they have pulled over, white or black, male or female, until they actually approach a car. Generally, traffic enforcement is focused on the act, not the actors.

"How ya doin', Officer Duke," the young man called as I approached the driver's door.

I immediately recognized the man as a local, who I'll call "John Norgood," (not his real name, because I can't remember it) whom I had seen and talked to many times at the Chevron station at Bolton Road and James Jackson Parkway. He usually drove a pickup truck and pulled a trailer filled with junk and recyclables. Today, he was in an older maroon two-door Lexus. He was about twenty-five years old and seemed to be very hard working and popular in the Riverside community of Atlanta. I later found out he was born and raised in Riverside and had extended family throughout the beat.

"I'm doing good, John, but I pulled you over because you were doing sixty-three on James Jackson Parkway. You know, the speed limit's only forty-five."

"Oh yeah, sorry about that. This is my mama's car, and I'm not used to it," he replied.

I went back and ran John's license on my MDT and was surprised to find he had a suspended license. I reviewed the data and saw that he did not have a Serve Date (notification from the court), so he may not have known that his license was suspended.

I walked back to his car, and asked, "John, did you know your license was suspended?"

After a short pause, he said, "No. What are you talking about?"

"Your license has been suspended by the courts. Did you know anything about that?"

"No, I had no idea," he said. "I can't imagine what it was for. Do you know?"

Sometimes, data from the MDT is very raw, with no explanation as to why a license is suspended, and such was the case this time. I could have done more digging and found the cause of the suspension, but now that he was in front of me, I could "serve" him myself by informing him about it.

"Tell you what we'll do," I said. "I'm not going to arrest you for driving while suspended, but I'm going to give you a ticket as proof that you have been warned about the suspension, plus a speeding ticket."

John started to protest, but I held up my hand, saying, "Listen, I'm doing you a favor; I'll reduce the speed to just fourteen miles over the limit. That way, you'll only have a small fine."

He acted disappointed but eventually signed the tickets. I let him park his car in a gas station parking lot, so it could be picked up later. I could have easily arrested him for the suspension and impounded his car, so he was getting a good break.

A few weeks later, at the same place, I clocked John doing twenty miles over the speed limit again.

"John, you know that your license is suspended. What in the world are you doing driving?" I asked.

Again, he acted totally surprised, saying there must be some kind of mistake. "You know, my daddy and I have the exact same name, maybe you got me confused with him," he started, as a way of explaining.

"No sir, I looked it up (on a web site that allows law enforcement to see the police record and a photo of the person in question), and it's definitely you who's got a suspended license. Also, I told you that your license was suspended a few weeks ago," I said.

"I know, but I got that all cleared up with a lawyer...if you'll just take me by the house, I can show you my paperwork," he argued.

He protested more as I put him in cuffs, saying, "You're really going to do this?"

"Yep, I'm really going to do this, this is my job," I said, trying to sound as sympathetic as possible. "Don't worry, if this is a mix-up, you can get it all straightened out with the courts today. Heck, you'll probably be home before I get off of work."

"Well, I never dreamed that you would treat me this way. You, of all people," he replied.

I really wasn't sure where he was going with that last comment, but later thought he may have been shocked that a white officer would arrest him.

We went back and forth like that—me, trying to sound sympathetic, and him trying to sound shocked at his treatment—but he finally settled down as we neared the city jail.

As we were parting at the jail, we both talked as if this was probably a big misunderstanding and it would be for the best, because he could get his license straightened out. Keep in mind, I knew that this wasn't a mistake, I had served him myself, and I knew that he knew it wasn't a mistake, but I kept up the charade in order to make the process as painless as possible.

When I got back into my car, I took the time to look and see if John had a criminal record. "Well, wouldn't you know it," I said out loud as I searched the crime data website. John had an extensive criminal record with two arrests for burglary and one conviction, several arrests for drugs, and two DUIs. And it was about to get a lot worse for him and several of the meth-heads in Riverside.

When I saw John at the Chevron a few weeks later, it seemed that all had been forgotten. He was very upbeat when we met, shaking my hand and telling me he was getting his life back together. He hadn't gotten his license fixed, but now he had his brother working with him and doing all the driving. Nonetheless, later that week I pulled him over for speeding again. This time, he was doing thirty miles per hour over the limit.

"John, I can't believe you're driving again," I said, with disappointment in my voice.

"Well, I was just taking my mom's car over to her house," he said, trying to force a smile.

As I leaned over to talk, I could smell alcohol on his breath. He failed the standardized field sobriety tests by a long shot. He was actually crying in the back of my police car as I took him back to city jail. I didn't see John again for many months, and when I did, it wasn't what I had expected.

In the meantime, while John was in jail, I arrested his brother for domestic violence and destruction of property and his father for an FTA warrant. His mom was present at both arrests, and she thought I was the Devil incarnate. I don't blame her; I had arrested her husband and a son and had arrested another son twice, all in a month's time.

Several months later, I got a call for a trespasser on a wooded lot out by some railroad tracks. The location was off the beaten path, and I had to take a muddy road to get within walking distance. As I approached, I could hear the sound of a bulldozer.

"Dang, John, what in the world are you doing way out here with a bulldozer," I exclaimed as I emerged from the woods.

John waved, shut down the engine, and jumped down to meet me.

"Oh, I'm doing some contract work for the owner. He wants me to clean up all these old tanks," he answered.

Swaying from the end of the bulldozer blade was a metal tank, probably about 250 gallons, like the kind you see next to homes that use oil for heating. I could see several more tanks in the brush, and I could see that John was moving them to a trailer close to the railroad tracks.

"Well, I got a complaint that someone was trespassing back here," I said as I went on to explain to him what had brought me out to the woods.

John's answers to my questions sounded plausible, so I called Dispatch for help: "2203 to Dispatch, could you call the key holder (complainant) and verify that Mr. John Norgood (not his real last name) is supposed to be out here working?"

A short time elapsed before the Dispatcher came back, saying, "The key holder said he's coming out to the site. ETA ten minutes."

I could immediately see John become uneasy when he heard that the owner of the property was on his way, and I thought he might try to make a run for it; however, I somewhat dismissed that idea when I realized he was wearing knee-high galoshes, and we were both standing in several inches of mud.

We made small talk as we waited, and John explained about how he was getting his life together. However, his mouth was having a hard time convincing his heart, and he eventually stopped talking and sat down to smoke a cigarette.

"He has to know that I've arrested his brother and father," I thought, as I stayed near to prevent an escape attempt.

The owner of the property arrived, and it quickly became apparent that John had not been contracted to clean up the tanks. The owner explained that each tank cost about $1,000 and would fetch $100 on the black market, and that he kept them at this location to keep them away from the prying eyes of thieves. He showed me invoices for the tanks and showed me where the property was marked for no trespassing. He pulled me aside and said that he was well acquainted with John, but that he had in no way hired him to clear up the tanks.

"Will you write out a victim statement?" I asked the owner.

"Damn right I will!"

I arrested John and later learned he was sentenced to a year in jail.

A year later, just days after getting out of jail, John was arrested again for driving on a suspended license. I learned about that case because John had given the officer, Officer Baker, my name and begged him to call me.

On the phone, Baker asked, "Do you know a guy named John Norgood?"

"Yeah, I know him. What's up?"

"Well, I just pulled him over for speeding and driving with a suspended license. I was thinking I'd cut him a break if you could vouch for him," he said.

"Yeah, I wish I could," I said. After a short pause, I asked, "Are his lips moving when he talks?"

Baker was laughing as he said, "Yep, they are definitely moving."

"Well then, anything he says when his lips are moving is probably a lie. Check Omnixx (crime history website). You'll see that this guy really doesn't deserve another break."

Another year later, John was arrested for stealing copper pipe from an old hospital on Bolton Road. In that case, he was caught red-handed as he was riding a bike, with twenty pounds of copper tubing, out of the hospital parking lot. At least he hadn't been driving a car.

I didn't see or hear about John while he was waiting to go to court for his copper case until, one afternoon, I was reading about a theft from a cement factory in Riverside. The police report said that the suspect had used a bulldozer to push away the dirt used to block a backroad into the factory compound. Then, the suspect had stolen two trailers with acetylene torch units on them. I knew that the factory was less than a quarter mile from where John lived, so I called the Zone 2 detective who had the case.

"Hey, I was reading about your cement factory case. I think I know who did it," I said to the detective over the phone.

He was interested and seemed excited to close the case within hours of opening it. I gave him some of John's history and told him he could probably find the stolen trailers in John's backyard.

Less than two hours later, at the end of my shift, I was greeted by a smiling detective who, after shaking my hand, thanked me, saying, "It was just like you said; they were in his backyard."

He proceeded to tell me how he'd gone over to John's place, saying, "Heck, he greeted me at the door as if I was a friend. He even said how he knew you, and y'all were friends. Then, he walked me around the house to show me he was innocent, and I found the trailers under a tarp."

"Is John here in the precinct?" I asked the detective.

"Yeah, he's over in the warrant room," he answered.

I walked over to the where John was, and he greeted me with a look of resignation. "I screwed up again, Officer Duke."

I let him tell me the details of his latest caper, and my heart really went out to him. I could tell he was trapped by alcohol and drugs in a life that was a revolving door to jail. Yes, he worked hard, and he could have been legitimately successful if it weren't for the demons chasing him. He seemed a broken man, and I wished I could do something to help him.

The law enforcement profession is filled with a lot of caring people who lift the downtrodden and give mercy to those who have made a mistake. Cops give mercy every day by warning people and giving them breaks if the crime is not too serious, like a traffic charge. But there comes a time when I cop has to be the bearer of bad news and force people to face justice. In John's case, there was nothing I could do except to wish him well and pray for him and his family.

John was not the only person on my beat that I had repeat run-ins with, but he's a good example of the problems faced by police. The recidivism rate for most crime is ridiculously high. Society has been throwing money at the problem for years, and crime "appears" to get worse. However, violent crime statistics are at an all-time low, more due to technology than social programs.

Most people believe that crime, and especially violent crime, is out of control, but FBI statistics indicate otherwise. Per the FBI's Uniform Crime Report system, violent crime in the United States has fallen to about half of what it was in 1993. Likewise, property crimes have fallen similarly since the early 1980's.

So, why do most people have the perception that crime is completely out of control? I can only speculate, but with the advent of 24-hour news stations—sometime in the mid-1980s—came a need for continuous information to fill their airwaves. In short, crimes that we used to never hear about, because they didn't occur near us and didn't involve anyone we knew, are now brought right into our living room around the clock.

In large part, I attribute technology to the drop in crime we've seen in the past two decades. As a small example, I can remember back in 1995, my boss at the time had purchased a "bag phone." (These were small phones you could plug into your cigarette lighter receptacle and get limited cell phone service. They wouldn't fit in a pocket, they were about the size of current walkie-talkies, so you'd sit them on something that resembled a bean-bag on the seat or drivetrain cover.) One day, the boss came into work, very excited, and told us how, on his way home the night before, he had witnessed a woman being assaulted. He said that as he drove up, the suspect took off running, and he had followed the suspect in his car and used his bag phone to call the police to the scene. Fast forward to the 21st century, where almost everyone has a smart phone, and it's easy to see that advances in technology have vastly improved crime reporting. There are literally millions of people, walking and riding around, who can contact the police and report a crime with just one button push; it's like having millions of extra police eyes.

Prior to the 1980's, most police had to be in their vehicles to use a radio, and the reception was limited to line-of-sight. Nowadays, police have mobile radios attached to their duty belts, using digital technology, which unties them from their vehicles and gives them a lot more options to thwart crime or pursue suspects. The suspect may be faster than the officer, but they'll never be faster than a radio.

The last ten years have brought huge improvements to security cameras. When I became a cop, most security camera footage was barely worth looking at, because the picture quality was so poor. Also, the cost of a good security system kept it out of reach for most small businesses and households. Five years later, technology brought the price down and improved the picture quality to the point that you could clearly identify a suspect with an inexpensive camera.

Combining improved camera technology and mobile communication with social media, text, instant messaging and emails, police and everyday citizens can get a clear photo or video of suspects to millions of people within minutes of a crime. People decry the "police state;" however, when placed into the hands of the entire population, it can be very effective. It's hard to cry "police state abuse" when it's controlled by millions of honest citizens. If you don't like it, don't commit crimes.

Enough's Enough

Despite my best efforts, after about three years on Beat 203, I started to get burned out. I had done just about everything imaginable to reduce crime on the beat; however, I found myself in the middle of a crime wave rolling in from Zone 1, just south of 203. Incidentally, Beat 203 is now a part of Zone 1; it's now Beat 103.

At some point, the gangs in Zone 1 discovered that the pickings were better in Zone 2. The cars had more expensive items in them, and the people were much less cautious and wary. So, car break-ins in Zone 2 climbed exponentially. It used to be that criminals just transited through 203 on their way to the rich northern neighborhoods. However, criminals would occasionally hit a vehicle in 203 as they retreated back to Zone 1.

Eventually, the criminals in Zone 1 discovered that the pickings were just as good in 203 as they were in the northern beats. In some cases, they were better, because the working-class people in 203 were more likely to keep weapons in their cars. I had one case where thieves stole five handguns out of a single pickup truck.

"I parked in front of the construction site and only went into the site for five minutes. When I came back to my truck, I found all of my guns gone!" the man said as he related the facts of the case to me.

"Was the vehicle locked?" I asked.

"No, I didn't lock it," the man answered, "I was only going into the site for five minutes."

I looked around. The man's truck was parked on a main street. Criminals like to target pickups for weapons. The suspects had probably been stalking the truck, saw the driver get out without locking it, and swooped in the minute he was out of sight. There were no cameras or witnesses in the area.

"So, you say he took all of your guns? How many guns did they take?" I asked, fully expecting to hear they'd taken two.

"Five," he said.

"Five guns?" I asked, thinking I might not have heard correctly.

"Yeah, they took all five guns. Handguns."

I paused for a minute and seriously considered just walking away; this guy was too dumb to warrant a police report. Instead, I did something even dumber, saying, "What in the hell were you doing with five handguns in your car?"

"Well, I went to the gun show last weekend, and I forgot that they were still in the truck," he answered.

"Sir, that is one of the most irresponsible statements I have ever heard. Do you realize that what you did will probably get someone shot or killed?" I said.

I immediately regretted what I said, not because the man was contrite, which he was, but because if he complained to the Department, I'd be in trouble with Internal Affairs.

"I'm so sorry," he said.

"Do you have the serial numbers for these weapons?"

"No, it was a private sale, and I didn't have time to write them down."

He went on to list the five guns, all of which were top of the line; a Sig Sauer, Glock, two Kimber's, and a Beretta.

My frustration and anger rose as I wrapped up the interview.

"Congratulations, Sir. You just armed the enemy. Way to go!" (I didn't actually voice this last comment, but I sure felt like saying it.)

In addition to a rising crime rate and frustration with the citizenry, I was becoming paranoid. Over the last three years, I'd arrested at least two hundred people on my beat. They didn't all live on the beat, which probably had a population of 10,000, but many did. I had arrested three generations of two different families and had arrested at least ten people more than once. This was all part of the job, but now I found myself running into these people all over the beat.

I used to be able to sit in the Chevron, at Bolton Road and James Jackson Parkway, and talk to the people; however, I found myself more and more having to look over my shoulder to see if someone was going to try and get revenge. It came to the point that the only place I could go to take a break was at Fire Station 8. That was nice, and they were happy to host me, but it wasn't what the beat needed. The beat needed someone who was engaged with the community.

I started to ask the sergeants for a beat change, but they urged me to stay in 203. I didn't want to sound like I was scared or shirking my duty, but I became desperate for a change. I went to the Administrative Sergeant at least twice and talked about it with the Sector Sergeant on several occasions. I even went to the Lieutenant; he told me to talk to the sergeants about it. It reminded me of going to my mother to ask for something and her saying, "Ask your father."

In order to document my request to change beats, I sent individual emails to the sergeants and Lieutenant, cc'ing my Sector Sergeant. Later, I sent them all a group email. I never got a written reply. Not one.

The only thing they would agree to do was make me a Roustabout, someone who worked whatever beat was open that day. But a Roustabout's schedule changes all the time, and I still ended up in 203 on a regular basis.

During this time, I started applying to other jobs around the Department. I applied with Narcotics, Red Dog, K9, Mounted Patrol, Planning and Research, Internal Affairs, Public Affairs, and the Aviation Unit, to no avail.

Making matters worse, my performance started to slip. I wrote the wrong charge on a ticket and had to go to court to get the charge thrown out. I found a woman at fault in an accident and was later shown, by a sergeant, that she wasn't at fault; again, I had to go to court and ask the judge to throw out the charge. But the worst thing was that I had three minor auto accidents within a year and a half. The last two were within five days of each other. I had never wrecked my own vehicles, not even a scratch, but here I was denting three police cars.

With mounting frustration, I made one last attempt to get an assignment change; I wrote an email to the Zone Commander, a major, requesting a new beat. Even though I Cc'd my Sector Sergeant and Lieutenant, they saw my actions as going outside of the chain of command. Within days, I was brought before the sergeants and given a written reprimand. But that wasn't the worst of it; they changed my off days from Sunday and Monday to Tuesday and Wednesday. I was livid

I had worked for a year and a half to get Sundays off, and here, with the swipe of a pen, it was gone. Sundays had become very special to my wife and me; it was the one day we got to spend together.

Trying to control my anger, I addressed the Administrative Sergeant: "You mean to tell me that after five years leading this zone in citations and arrests, and after three years of cleaning up the biggest and worst beat in the zone, you are going to take my off days away?"

He answered with a simple, "Yes."

I saluted smartly and left the office.

I broke the bad news to my wife, and she was all for me just resigning. However, I loved police work, and it had become my identity. Also, I knew there was some place I could serve where my work would be appreciated, and I'd be supported. I truly loved the Atlanta Police Department, and I wasn't about to let this ruin that for me, or the Department. Unfortunately, I had been hit by forces beyond my control. One of those forces didn't become apparent to me until over a year later.

At first, I tried to continue just as I had before, being aggressive and chalking up my mistakes, and the consequences, to bad timing. I reckoned, "In every life some rain must fall." However, it became quickly apparent that my heart wasn't into it. Before long, I found myself just going through the motions. My ticket average fell from five a day to two a week. My arrests went from two a week to two a month. In addition, I hid in the fire station or in a secluded place until I got dispatched to a call. Even then, I went to my calls reluctantly and started to hate my job.

Just when I was at my lowest, a few days before Christmas, with plans to resign in the new year, I got a lifeline.

When I had interviewed with Planning and Research, the commander of the unit, Lt. Ablan, had introduced me to his boss, Major Quigley. During our discussion, I told him that in the Air Force I had worked in European Command Headquarters, J-9, Plans and Programs.

"Officer Duke, your work experience would be perfect for this job," Major Quigley said. He went on to tell me he'd worked in European Command with the Army. He knew what my job entailed. "The problem is, it's very hard for us to get people from the zones. But I'll see what I can do to get you in Planning and Research."

A year passed. By now, I was resigned to my fate in Zone 2. Nonetheless, out of the blue, my Administrative Sergeant called me to say I was being transferred. I was to report in a week.

I remember quite vividly what I was doing when I found out I was being transferred: I was sitting on a side street, doing some paperwork, when I saw a young man skateboarding down the sidewalk. "Wow, that's nice. You don't see too many kids skateboarding around here. He's not very good at it, but at least he's trying," I thought.

Five minutes later, a gentleman ran out of the parking deck across the street, and up to my car, shouting, "You need to come, someone has stolen from my car!"

I drove into the parking deck and saw the man's car door hanging open. Next to the car was a skateboard.

"I came out of the gym, and there was this kid going through my car. He ran that way," the man said as he pointed towards the back of the garage.

I ran towards the back, and my phone started vibrating. I continued to run, rounded a corner, and saw a big dumpster. I ran behind the dumpster and found the skateboarder just standing there. My phone vibrated again.

"I was just smoking a cigarette," he said as I turned him around and put cuffs on him.

"Smoking, huh?" I remarked as I searched his pockets. "You don't even have any cigarettes."

"I was going to borrow a smoke," he replied.

My phone vibrated again.

As I pulled keys to a Dodge Charger from his pocket, he said, "Oh, those ain't mine. Someone gave them to me."

"Who gave it to you?"

"Oh, just some dude I met. I swear to God!"

"Just some dude. What's he look like?" I asked.

We went back and forth about his alibi, and I realized that my phone had been vibrating the entire time. Finally, after getting the kid into the back of my patrol car, I took the time to see who had been calling me; it was the Administrative Sergeant.

Christmas and New Year's flew by, and I reported to Planning, Research and Accreditation (PRAU) on January 2nd.

PRAU was a much-needed break. Lieutenant Ablan warned me that transitioning from the street would take a few weeks and, at the time, I thought he was exaggerating. He wasn't.

It took about two months for me to get comfortable being in an office. I was constantly looking around and checking out my tactical situation. They put me in the middle of a big room of office cubicles, and I was nervous to the point of fatigue for several weeks.

I enjoyed my work in headquarters but came to the quick realization that there wasn't enough work to keep all of us busy. The majority of the people were great, and many were there because, like me, they were burnt out from the streets. However, I became acquainted with a new breed of cop, the kind that like the idea of being an officer but don't want to actually be a cop. I met several of these "cops" who bragged about being at headquarters for ten, fifteen, and some over twenty years.

Not only had these people been there a long time, they didn't accomplish anything while they were there. They had perfected the art of looking busy but not actually being busy. If you asked them for something, they'd put you off by insinuating that their schedule was really busy. After a few weeks, if you asked again, they'd come up with some other excuse. One of these cops was in charge of Georgia State accreditation for the Department. He put in his resignation, so State accreditation was given to me. I asked him several times to go over the State files with me, but he always had something more pressing. Eventually, he was gone, and I was stuck to figure it out on my own.

I had been doing National accreditation, so I wasn't too worried that State accreditation would be a problem; I dove into the files. Unfortunately, there were no files to dive into, and I hit the bottom of the pool. Sure enough, when I looked to see what he'd accomplished so far that year, I found that he had done absolutely nothing. Even worse, he had done nothing the year before. I was stuck going back a year and a half and doing the things he should have been doing all along. It took me six months.

My two years at Headquarters was a great break. But I was eager to go back to real policing.

Chapter 16. APD Sergeant

Welcome to Zone 3

I arrived for my first duty day as a sergeant at the old house used as the precinct headquarters for Atlanta's Zone 3--a dilapidated two-story adjacent to Zoo Atlanta--about an hour before Night Watch roll call. As I pulled into a parking spot, another vehicle was pulling into the spot just across from me. When the driver emerged, I noticed he was wearing sergeant's stripes.

"Sergeant Lynch?" I said, as I walked towards him.

"Yes, sir!" he said, raising his voice as he emphasized "sir" and extended his hand.

"Do you go by William, Bill, or Lynch?" I asked, with some hesitation—seeing that he was thinking about the question.

"Call me William or Lynch. Bill is my dad's name," he replied.

I knew, right then, that I was dealing with a solid guy.

We walked towards the precinct, but Lynch pulled up to a smaller building behind the house, saying, "Evening Watch and Night Watch offices are in here."

I followed him through a messy storage area, lined with old lockers, to a back room with four adjacent offices, each the size of a small bedroom. The main room had a counter running through the center of it, but it was covered with paper, old equipment and assorted office supplies.

"This is our office," he said, as he unlocked a rickety door and led me into a room with three old desks and a tall filing cabinet. "Just pick a desk."

I sat down at the desk with the smallest computer monitor. The computer was an older model, the same model as those replaced at headquarters several years earlier. "I see you guys have the latest equipment," I said, in an attempt at humor.

"Yep, nothing but the best for Zone 3," he replied.

As I got situated, I thought back to the many times I had done this same ritual in the Air Force. During that time, in all of my twelve job moves, all but one of my office buildings was older than me. However, the Air Force outfitted us with the latest equipment, and the buildings, though old, were renovated and clean. The Zone 3 offices looked like the City had just taken over an abandoned house, thrown the supervisors in the garage, and bought the furniture and equipment from yard sales.

"So, how long have you been in Zone 3?" I asked Lynch.

He looked up, as if he were searching for an answer, and said, "Just a month; I made sergeant a month ago."

We talked a little more, and I discovered that Lynch had been in police academy Class 213, two classes behind me in Class 211. It was reassuring to see that this confident guy had about the same experience level as I did—maybe I'd be just as confident in a month.

Sergeant Lynch let me observe him as he prepared for the first roll call. When we walked into the roll call room, located in the main house, I was struck by how young the officers were. I called the officers to line up, and did the equipment inspection. Lynch briefed them on what had gone on earlier in the day, personnel issues, and the areas we needed to concentrate on overnight.

After the second roll call, at 11 p.m., Lynch drove me around the zone, highlighting some high crime areas and things to look for. Sometime during our drive, while talking about violent crimes, I asked Lynch how many murders had occurred during the four weeks he'd been in the zone. "Oh, I'd say about eight," he answered.

"Eight! You've got to be kidding me!" I replied. "I didn't have that many in the seven years I was in Zone 2."

Again, Lynch looked upward, searching his memory, and said, "Yep. I think it's exactly eight."

I racked my brain trying to recall murders during my years patrolling Zone 2, and I could come up with only two, and one of those had happened when I wasn't on duty.

"Eight?"

"Eight," he replied.

"Eight murders in four weeks?"

"Yes, sir. Eight murders. Thankfully, these guys aren't good shots, because I'd say there are eight to ten shootings or stabbings for every one murder."

I sat in stunned silence for a moment, and then Lynch told me that virtually all the shootings were due to a recent gang war which had been going on in south Atlanta for the last several months. Little did I know, I'd be faced with this lethal reality before sunrise.

The hot and humid night air was an apt accompaniment for the beginning of the shift as the 911 Dispatcher moved our beat cars to emergencies throughout the zone. Most of the calls were for property crimes like vandalism and burglary. However, a large number were crimes against persons-- fights, shots fired, robberies, and domestic disputes. This stood in contrast to the crimes I faced as an officer in north Atlanta, where the vast majority were property crimes.

As I listened to the police radio, I thought about the young people I'd seen in roll call--almost half of them women--going to these potentially violent calls, not knowing what they would encounter or what they'd be called on to do. Lynch and I backed up a few of the officers on calls, and the officers appeared confident and able to handle themselves.

After a couple of hours, Lynch and I went back to the precinct. He went to the office, and I headed back out into the zone. With my smart-phone and map, I tried to get my bearings in this unknown part of the city.

I pulled out my map and had just started orienting myself to the main roads when, breaking through my concentration, the voice of a Dispatcher reported a shooting at an apartment complex on Metropolitan Avenue.

Knowing it would be faster, I threw the map aside, pulled out my phone, and said, "Okay, Google, navigate me to 675 Metropolitan Parkway."

Google answered with, "Alright. 675 Metropolitan Parkway S-W. Let's go."

I arrived at the apartment complex within a few minutes and found several officers already there and police tape going up. I parked outside of the complex, checked in with an officer manning the entry checkpoint, and walked down to where three police cars were parked with their blue lights on. Although body cameras were entirely new to me, I had the presence of mind to make sure mine was recording.

Officer Mahler (not his real name) turned towards me as I approached.

"What you got?" I asked, trying to sound more confident than I actually was. In fact, I was anything but confident. I could feel my body trembling slightly as Mahler walked me towards a minivan with its sliding doorframe showcasing a young man sprawled across the back seat.

"Looks like he was only hit once," Mahler said as he pointed a flashlight beam toward the man's left hip. "There's tons of blood, but we can only find one entry wound. Must have hit the femoral."

"Yeah, the (Old Been There Done That) femoral," I replied, trying to sound like I'd seen it all before.

"He was shot in the parking garage; it's a bloody mess up there, and it looks like a friend grabbed him, threw him into the van to rush him to the hospital, and when he came out of the garage, he saw us, slammed brakes, jumped out of his vehicle, ran around the front and threw open the door…" Mahler said.

Other officers had gathered around, and one of them interrupted, saying, "Yeah, he's lucky we didn't shoot him. He came flying right towards us, and then slammed on his brakes and jumped out."

"We threw-down on him until it became clear he wasn't a threat," a third officer added.

"Where is the friend?" I asked.

"Over there," someone replied, pointing a flashlight towards a patrol car with an open door and an officer standing next to it, talking to someone in the back seat.

Within a few minutes, a General Investigator (GI), Grady Bus, and the Night Captain were on scene. I let the officers continue doing what they obviously had done may times before; make the area safe, gather witnesses, and otherwise help the investigators. I walked over to the scene of the shooting, in the parking garage, and was amazed at how much blood could come out of a human body. There had to be at least a half-gallon painting the garage floor. I could see where the victim originally fell and could make out the slide marks where the friend had dragged the body to the van. There had also been a lot of blood on the van floor, so it was obvious the victim had bled out right after being put in the van.

I tried to see if I could find any witnesses, but everyone retreated back into their buildings when they saw me approaching. I knocked on a few doors, but no one answered. I made some phone calls to let my superiors know what had happened and spent the next two to three hours keeping watch over the scene in the parking garage as Homicide detectives did their investigation.

About two hours into the investigation, as I was standing guard at the scene, ten to fifteen shots rang out from no more than 100 yards away, on the other side of the parking garage. Immediately, two female officers ran to their patrol cars and headed towards the shots. (I mention the fact they were female to illustrate that all officers do the same job, regardless of gender). The officers later reported they'd found 5.56 mm casings in a street just outside the apartment complex, no victims.

The on-scene investigation wound down, and the general consensus was that this was a drug deal gone bad. "Luckily, we've got a cooperating witness," I heard a homicide detective say.

As the detective's words resonated, I heard Dispatch report a shooting on the south end of the zone. Strangely, the address given was 180 Southside Industrial Boulevard, the address of the Atlanta Police Department's training academy. I ran towards my vehicle, a Ford Expedition, and headed south.

There wasn't much talk on the radio as my mind raced with, "What in the world could have happened at the Academy? Is this a bogus call? Could it be a training event and some trainee called on the wrong frequency?"

As I turned off the highway, about a half-mile from the Academy, I saw police cars at a gas station on Browns Mill Road.

"Looks like the shooting occurred over on Jonesboro Road, 1313 is over there now," an officer reported. (To designate a patrol officer on the radio, Night Watch units use 13 and then a two-digit beat number; the 1 represents the first watch of the day, and the 3 denotes the zone. Therefore, 1313 is the radio number for Night Watch, Zone 3, Beat 13. Supervisors are numbered in the 90s; the Watch Commander, a lieutenant, is 91, so his radio number is 1391. We sergeants get the other numbers in no particular order. My radio number was 1395. Zone 3 Day Watch units use a prefix of 23, and Evening Watch uses 33).

The victim's car, sitting in the parking lot between the gas pumps and the store, had a blown tire and a couple of bullet holes in a rear quarter-panel. Nearby, two women and a man were talking with an officer.

"Those were the passengers in the car," an officer said, pointing in the direction of the people being interviewed. "Looks like they got in a shootout over on Jonesboro. The victim was the driver. They said he was trying to make it to the hospital but pulled in here instead."

Just then, a skinny middle-aged white woman came up, seemingly out of nowhere, saying, "How can that guy still be alive, he had a bullet hole right in his stomach?"

She hesitated, and I just stared at her, wondering where she'd come from, and then she said, "He walked right in the store and lifted his shirt and said 'Call 911'." The woman provided a visual aid by pulling up the front of her shirt. I later learned she was a homeless person who hung around the store and did odd jobs in exchange for food.

The woman continued to explain how surreal the situation was, except she didn't use the word "surreal." Meanwhile, the three passengers had obviously finished their interview with the officer, and they were demanding to get their "things" out of the car. "I'm sorry," was one officer's reply, "This vehicle is now part of a crime scene."

"Well, this is bulls#!t! We didn't do nothin', and you gonna just treat us like we guilty..." one of the women protested.

Another officer leaned over to me and whispered, "We can see at least one pistol under the driver's seat."

I took that as my cue to say something. "Ma'am, I'm sorry, but we have to wait for crime scene technicians to come and process the car."

The threesome continued to voice their complaints, as if we'd just relent and say, "Oh, okay, you can go in the car and retrieve your guns before we begin processing the car."

Suddenly, as if on cue, each of them started walking separately around the scene, trying to get a better view of the inside of the car. We let them approach but not close enough to see what we could see on the car floor.

The story evolved as we investigated. It appeared that this group had gotten into an altercation with another group at a gas station on Jonesboro Road. Video evidence showed that the other group started shooting, and the group we were with started shooting back. The other group drove out of the gas station but ran into a fence and fled on foot. This group had driven off, and one of them thought that there would be medical or police assistance at the Academy, at 3 o'clock in the morning, so they had Googled it:

'Hey, Google, take me to the nearest police!"

"Alright. Atlanta Police Training Academy. Let's go."

Apparently, they had been disappointed at the Academy and subsequently dialed 9-1-1. They told 9-1-1 they were going to try to make it to the hospital, but the driver decided he couldn't make it without some help, so he stopped at this gas station. The Grady Bus (ambulance) had already left with the victim before I got there. We later heard that the victim was in stable condition; he was going to make it.

By the end of the week, Homicide had identified all the suspects in the murder of the man on Metropolitan Parkway and had three people in custody. Furthermore, the Department had identified most of the people in the gas station shooting and had at least two under arrest.

My wife was cheerfully waiting for me when I got home from my first shift in Zone 3.

"How did it go?" she asked.

I gave her the highlights of what had happened.

"Well, do you think you're going to like it? she asked.

"Yes, I think I will."

In my first five days in Zone 3 Night Watch there were ten shootings, one stabbing, and three people died as a result. Add that to the robberies, auto accidents, burglaries, fights, alarms, thefts and suicides, and it made for one really busy week. As I heard on more than one occasion, "Welcome to Zone 3."

Adjusting to Reality

Life as a sergeant was proving to be a harder adjustment for me than I thought it be. I had been a very aggressive officer and often found myself, in the first few weeks, thinking like a patrol officer—I'd see an infraction and immediately respond. However, this got me into some tough binds, because if there was more to the case than I first surmised, I'd find myself bogged down with paperwork, tow trucks, and reports. For instance, if I pulled someone over for a simple moving violation and found out the driver was unlicensed, the stop could turn from a ten-minute ticket session into two hours of investigation, waiting for a tow truck, taking the violator to jail, and writing a report.

As a patrol officer, cases like this are what you want; it's the reason you're on the street; the bigger the better. But as a sergeant, my job was to direct the watch and help it be as efficient as it could be. Getting bogged down with cases could be detrimental to getting the watch functioning at full capacity.

Several weeks after arriving at Zone 3, I was looking over the productivity of our officers and was surprised to discover several of them, almost half, hadn't written a single proactive traffic citation in the last month. Some of them had gone over six weeks without a citation. (A proactive citation is one written from a traffic stop, not from an accident or other road incident.)

I shook my head in amazement. "How can you go weeks without writing a citation?" was my thought. I spent well over half of the shift on the streets and had written about ten tickets in the last four weeks, without even trying. You only had to sit somewhere by the road and in less than five minutes a violation would pass by—no tag, no lights, speeding.

A few of the officers were getting two or three citations per shift, so I knew it was possible to be productive in Zone 3 Night Watch. Additionally, I had worked crime scenes with these officers and knew they were industrious and willing to work. So why was almost half of our shift not producing?

I brought up the lack of productivity with the other sergeants, and there were several theories as to why Night Watch was underperforming: The officers are lazy, scared, or incompetent, were just some of the theories we discussed.

Traffic stops are a proven crime prevention technique. Officers who routinely made traffic stops were often rewarded with finding out the driver had a warrant, or discovering drugs and illegal guns in the car. Of course, these discoveries rewarded the officers with more work, which supports the "lazy" theory of why officers weren't doing traffic stops.

In nightly roll calls, we urged the officers to be more aggressive, with no success. Occasionally they would have a good week and have a lot of citations and arrests to show for it. Normally, Night Watch would have fifty to seventy traffic citations, well below what the other watches were getting. It would be several more weeks before we discovered the primary cause.

I Heard You Hunt Sharks

Criminals don't think like you and I do (unless you're a criminal). We see a nice car and we think to ourselves, "Wow! That's a nice car. I'd sure love to ride in something like that." In contrast, a criminal sees a nice car and thinks, "Wow! That's a nice car. I need to break into it; I'm sure there's something in there I can use or sell." It's a totally different mindset. That's why you'll often hear average citizens, and even cops, say, "That just doesn't make any sense," when they are exposed to certain crimes.

Most urban crime happens in the poorer parts of town against the struggling families that live in that part of town. To me, it doesn't make any sense that night after night young men and women are looking to victimize other men and women who are a lot like them. Of course, it doesn't make sense to me; I'm not a criminal.

I believe that most criminals learn their skills by how they are brought up. For instance, one of the most critical "skills" to becoming a successful criminal is to be able to lie with conviction. Most children go through a short, what I'll call "Lying Stage," when they are quite young, somewhere between three and six years old. In this stage, they may find out that a small lie gets them off the hook when they misbehave. "It wasn't me! The dog ate the cookies."

In this case, if the child has good and attentive parents, they will eventually see through the kid's lies and put a stop to it. Sure, it may work once or twice, but eventually a loving parent will correct the child's behavior. However, if a child doesn't have adequate parental guidance, and the parents don't have the will or time to correct the child, the child will learn that lying works. Confidence in their ability to lie is what the blossoming criminal relies on to give courage to commit the infraction and the skill to get away with it.

Another "skill" that aids criminals is the inclination to act on impulse, not through thoughtful consideration. The window to commit most crimes is usually very small, maybe only a second or two, and criminals know they have to act quickly. "Quick, grab that beer from the cooler before the store clerk looks this way," or, "The lady just got out of the car and left it running while she went into the convenience store—get in that car and go!" Worse yet, "He disrespected me! BOOM! Bust a cap in that ass!" Again, acting on impulse pays off for the criminal in the short run, because they don't have to think about doing it; they just do whatever impulse comes to mind.

Let's face it, children are compulsive, and breaking compulsion in favor of thoughtful consideration is what maturing is all about. If a child has someone around to help them curb their impulses and model good behavior, like a parent or mentor, they are much less likely to resort to crime when they are older.

Finally, young people who don't have parents or a community to motivate them to learn, do well in school, and take pride in a job well done, end up with few, if any, marketable skills with which to make a living when they are older. Therefore, crime often becomes the best, or only, option they see to a better life.

I can remember the times my father said, "After you graduate, you had better be in college or have a job, because you ain't living here." That may seem cruel, but my father said those things as a warning: Get your act together, because one day you'll be on your own. I clearly recall about two years after graduation (when I had a job, a two-room apartment, and an old car) thinking, "I can support myself; I'm going to make it." It felt great.

A lot of people think poverty is the biggest motivator to a criminal. I don't think so. There are many examples of people who were raised in abject poverty and never committed a serious crime. Oprah Winfrey was raised dirt poor on a farm in Mississippi, studied and got a college scholarship, became a TV correspondent, and went on to become one of the richest and most popular people in the world. Shahid Khan immigrated from Pakistan as a young man and worked as a dishwasher before working his way to success. He is now the owner of a large company, the Jacksonville Jaguars football team, and a Premier League soccer club. Ursula Burns was raised in the projects but eventually rose to CEO of Xerox. What did all these people have in common other than poverty? They all had at least one person who cared enough to consistently teach them right from wrong and to hold them accountable. And I could name you a dozen or more top-notch police officers who came from very poor childhoods. On the other hand, I know of many people who were very well off, and they still became criminals.

Charles Ponzi came from a wealthy Italian family, and he scammed people out of millions; I know you've heard of a Ponzi Scheme. John Dillinger was the son of a middle-class grocer but became a robber, murderer, and the FBI's Enemy Number One. Herman Mudgett, AKA H.H. Holmes, was raised in affluence, went to medical school, and eventually became a pharmacist; he was also America's first known serial killer. Bernie Madoff was the son of a well-to-do stockbroker, yet ruined countless lives and caused massive damage. Sure, it's a factor, but poverty never created a criminal; bad upbringings and a lack of accountability are the primary factors.

To give credit where it's due, lack of money plays a part in that many families are torn apart by poverty. In some cases, parents will leave, or be forced to leave, the family because they can't provide for the children's needs. Some parents have been known to abandon their families, because it was too much work to take care of the kids with limited means. Yes, in these instances, poverty played a role; however, if the parent had been raised to take pride in themselves, work hard, and strive to help others, they would have probably found a way to provide for their children and bring them up with the same good attributes.

With these elements; the ability to lie and poor impulse control, a culture that celebrates gangsters, no marketable work skills, and parents who are either not there or don't care, a young person is well on their way to becoming a career criminal.

I have been one of those people who said or thought, "That just doesn't make sense!" when I see some of the thing's criminals do. However, as a police officer working in the streets, you don't have much time to spend figuring out why criminals do things. You have to prevent it, respond to it, and/or deal with the consequences.

Regardless of what motivates criminals, I often think they act a lot like sharks. A shark spends most of its time nosing around for something to eat. Sharks bump into things, almost anything, and when they perceive it as food, they take a bite. If it's good, they eat it. If not, they move on. Sure, they might bite the occasional surfer, but eventually they'll bite into something that satisfies their hunger. At least for a little while.

You're probably thinking, "Dude, that's harsh!" I say, "No, that's reality." At least that's a reality I can keep in mind when I'm at work, allowing me to better understand and predict their unpredictable behavior.

When I'm not at work, I enjoy my family and friends. We give back to our community through charity, church, volunteering, taking care of our responsibilities, and respecting the rights of others. In contrast, criminals go through their day looking for what they can get from others. They lack the skills to do a real job, no one can trust them because they are accomplished liars, and their lack of impulse control gives them the opportunity to act without thinking of the consequences. To deal with that mindset, it helps me to be able to put things into some perspective (visualizing criminal behavior as being similar to a shark's), even if my model is not 100% accurate.

Last Days

A major frustration I had in Zone 3 was rooted in what I perceived as officers' unwillingness to patrol the zone assertively. Crime and probable cause were all over the place, yet many of our officers appeared to be oblivious to it.

Arrests made by law enforcement are based on the theory of Probable Cause (PC). PC can be defined as: That set of facts or circumstances that would lead a reasonable person to believe that a crime has been, or is about to be, committed, and that the person in question is involved in a significant manner. It is more than mere speculation, but less than actual certainty.

If a law enforcement officer has PC to believe someone has committed, or is about to commit a crime, they are justified to make an arrest. PC is the life-blood of law enforcement. When an officer is not responding to PC, or dealing with the consequences, their job is to search for PC and act upon it. Cops don't have to be certain or be convinced beyond a reasonable doubt; that's for the courts. Cops need PC to make an arrest.

Nightly, I implored the Watch to search for PC and act on it. And nightly, most of them didn't. I even tried to help some of them out by seeing the crime and leading them to it. For instance, I'd see people soliciting in the street and call the beat officer to investigate. Or, I'd pull someone over for a tag violation, and I'd call an officer to handle it. Mind you, I only did this when we weren't busy, usually between around two-thirty and four-thirty a.m. And I only called underperforming officers. That usually only produced one arrest and one pissed-off officer.

Hurting officers' feelings because they were screwing up didn't bother me much; however, it hurt morale, and that did bother me. So, I eventually eased off and tried to be as observant as possible.

One night, I was listening to the radio and it dawned on me how well our officers backed each other up on calls. It seemed that no matter the call, there was always someone volunteering to backup that officer. Had I not been in the Zone for a few months, I might have seen this as officers just looking to burn a few unproductive hours before the end of their shift. But Zone 3 was different. Zone 3 was violent and unpredictable; death could come in many forms very fast if you weren't prepared. All but three of my nights in Zone 3 involved shootings.

I began to understand why many officers weren't getting traffic tickets and arrests; they were concerned that if they were busy with a minor arrest, they wouldn't be available to back up a fellow officer in need. This helped me understand the forces working on the shift. Of course, some of the officers were just lazy and didn't want to do anything. However, most of the underperforming officers were just trying to look out for their brothers and sisters in blue.

Later, as I was studying the roll call rosters from other watches, my theory was strengthened. In looking at the Day and Evening Watch rosters, I saw that all but maybe one or two of their beats had an officer in them on almost every shift. Furthermore, they always had an administrative officer and usually had a paddy wagon, special traffic officers, and umbrella officers covering the entire zone.

On Night Watch, we pulled beats almost every night, averaging two or three a shift, because we didn't have enough bodies to fill them. We only had an administrative officer if someone had to be on light duty. We never had a paddy wagon, traffic officer, or umbrella officer. We were desperately short, sometimes pulling five of our thirteen beats, leaving just eight officers to cover thirteen beats. In short, we didn't have the manpower to do the job effectively.

Most of our better performing officers were in the northern part of the zone, A-Sector. One of the reasons they were more productive is that they worked together, during slow times, to get tickets and make arrests. It was very common for two or three of them to go out on the highway together and catch speeders.

For example, Officer Francisco (not his real name) and Officer Mahler would regularly coordinate with each other on the zone's secondary radio channel and make several traffic stops in less than an hour. They also made a lot of arrests. The key was, they were together. If one of them got dispatched to a call, the other one would go as backup, if possible.

While talking to the other sergeants, I found that they were in agreement about our shortage of officers and what we could do about it. As a result, we started stressing the idea of working together. We went a step farther by moving officers around so that they could learn teamwork from A-Sector units.

This teamwork helped get our productivity up, but the biggest boost was when we got four new officers on the Watch. Three of the officers came from the academy and one transferred over from Evening Watch. In addition, many of our officers returned from extended military duty or medical leave. Suddenly, we were able to fill our beats and have one or two officers available for special duties. Additionally, if we knew someone wasn't getting traffic stops, we'd make them the Traffic Car; all they needed was ten citations to have a successful shift. We still didn't have the available manpower of the other watches, but we had enough people to have an effective watch. As great as all this was, I didn't really get a chance to enjoy it, because I made another discovery.

End of Watch

One evening my wife and I were going over our finances, looking forward to retirement somewhere in the next three to five years. The more we looked, the more we realized how good our finances were. For most of my post Air Force career, the economy had really suffered and so had the stock market. Now, the economy was booming and so was our investment portfolio. We had saved money quite well and realized that I could retire anytime I wanted, and we'd be in good shape.

I had concerns about retiring because I loved my job, and being a cop had become a big part of my life, my identity; very similar to how being a pilot had been my identity in the Air Force.

"But David, you're always complaining about the commute," my wife, Linda, reminded me.

Yes, the dreadful commute; forty-nine miles each way, and I had to use the Interstate 75/85 connector. I had to admit, that commute was a killer.

As I sat there pondering whether or not to retire, Linda had a brilliant idea. "Let's do this; let's experiment with retirement," she said.

"Experiment? How do you experiment with it? You're either retired or you're not," I said.

"Well, let's just say we'll retire at the end of the month, and act as if it's a fact for one week," she said.

"One week? How does that work?"

"We'll just agree, right here and now, that we're retiring in three weeks, and see how that sits with us. If, after a week, we're not comfortable with it, we'll just keep on working," she said, raising her pitch at the end of the sentence as if to say, "It's no big deal."

I was doubtful but agreed to go along with her idea. That night I slept better than I had in years; ten hours solid (actually I slept during the day and worked at night, but you get my drift). The next few days, I became more and more sold on the idea of retiring. By the fourth day, I had made up my mind; I'd retire at the end of the month.

The next few weeks crawled by as I counted down to retirement. Fortunately, we were seeing real improvements in performance, and I could sense that something good was happening on Night Watch. Of course, we still had challenges, and there was one officer still butt-hurt that I didn't let her do whatever she wanted whenever she wanted (skip roll call, not cover her beat, not do any proactive policing, be disrespectful and rude, stuff like that).

We got a new sergeant on the watch during my last week, Sergeant Corey Kornbacher. I knew from the first words out of his mouth that he would fit in very well with Sergeant Lynch and Sgt Wall's aspirations for Night Watch.

"I think everything's going to be alright," was one of the last things I said to Sergeant Lynch as I left work for the last time.

Although we wanted to see our traffic numbers improve, we viewed that as just one measure of how we were doing our job. Most of all, we wanted our officers to love law enforcement as much as we did. To us, the only way you'll ever love your job is to be good at it, and that involves hard work.

I believe being a law enforcement officer is the most noble and important profession in the world. If you live in or near a big city, you need the police like pancakes need syrup. In any large city, if the police were to announce a one-week break in service, that city would cease to be a functioning entity by the end of that week. It would take a callout of the National Guard to return some semblance of order.

I loved my years of military service, but I did more good (for my community and the nation) in my first year as a police officer than in the twenty-three years I served in the United States Air Force. I was a rescue pilot in the Air Force and was credited with twelve "Saves" during my career; however, over 90% of my time in the Air Force was spent in training. As a police officer, over 95% of my time was spent in active police work, serving the citizens and protecting the community from crime. Those twelve "Saves" I had in the

Air Force were important, but I can't even begin to count how many people I saved from death, injury, despair, hunger, cold, and victimhood as a police officer. I'm not bragging; ask any good law officer and they'll tell you something very similar.

Two weeks into retirement, as I was typing this book, I got an email from Zone 3 with the latest traffic numbers. The email was originally sent out by the Zone 3 Commander. The top of the attached report had a picture of the actor Will Farrell dressed as TV news anchor Ron Burgundy, with the caption, "BREAKING NEWS: YOU'RE ALL AWESOME!" Below that were the results of traffic enforcement from the preceding week. It showed Day Watch with 108 stops, Evening Watch with 149, and Morning (Night) Watch with 142.

Only once had I seen Night Watch with more than 100 traffic stops (103 stops), and I had never seen them surpass another watch. This was great news. MORE BREAKING NEWS: ATLANTA POLICE DEPARTMENT, YOU'RE SO MONEY, YOU DON'T KNOW HOW MONEY YOU ARE!

Prologue

Police work has changed considerably since I first published Notes in Blue less than a year ago. The demands on law enforcement have dramatically increased due to the emergence of COVID-19 and increased social unrest. Now, law enforcement officers (LEOs) have to not only worry about criminals, they have to take measures to protect themselves and others from a dangerous virus. Furthermore, increased public scrutiny, actions that limit force options, and liability issues force many LEOs into untenable situations that put their lives and the lives of citizens at risk.

Many citizens and politicians are calling for defunding the police or reducing funding for law enforcement. I believe this will have an effect opposite of that intended. Reducing funds will decrease police presence, increase response times, and reduce the tools needed to deal with certain situations. Furthermore, LEOs are already underpaid and if their pay is further decreased, it will be harder to hire good officers.

Increased scrutiny of police officers is important; however, if civic leaders charge officers for crimes in order to meet the demands of citizens who may not know the facts of the case, officers will be wrongly accused. Arresting officers based solely on public demand makes for a situation that no LEO wants. If unwarranted arrests become the norm, the quality of police recruits will decline, and on-duty officers may just look the other way instead of doing their jobs. When a LEO is arrested or charged with a crime, it is always front-page news. What kind of person will law enforcement attract if there's a high likelihood they will be falsely accused and charged with a crime? The answer is simple: desperate people who can't find any other job. Is that the kind of people we want in law enforcement? If it is, then many large cities in the United States are well on their way to getting it.

Make no mistake, reductions in law enforcement spending will affect people in poor communities more than those who live in affluent areas. People with the means to do so will hire their own private police if they feel their city is not providing adequate police protection.

Law enforcement agencies and their members are not perfect; what group of humans is? Cutting funding and increasing law enforcement's civil and criminal liability is not going to improve police procedure. I don't know what the future holds for law enforcement, but I know that cutting funding and wrongfully charging officers with crimes will not improve it.

I loved being a LEO, but I'm glad I retired before Defund the Police became popular.

About the author:

David Allen Duke was raised an Army brat, moving with his family twenty-one times by the age of twenty-two. He served for twenty-three years as a pilot in the U.S. Air Force, moving his own family twelve times. He's a husband, father, and grandfather. He lives with his wife in north Georgia and spends his time riding motorcycles, fishing, and bothering her. This is his first book.

☐

Made in the USA
Columbia, SC
22 March 2021